Buying and Leasing Cars on the Internet

Ron Raisglid

with William Mikulak and Cheri Turner

BOOKS

Renaissance Books
Los Angeles

Visit the Renaissance Books Web site for information on other exciting titles:
www.renaissancebks.com

Grateful acknowledgment is made to the following Web sites for permission to
reproduce their graphics in this book: Autobytel.com, AutoSite, BanxQuote,
Cadillac, Car and Driver, Carfax, CarWizard, Classifieds2000, Edmund's,
Equifax, GEICO Direct, Insurance News Network, InsWeb, Kelley Blue Book,
LINC Acceptance Company, MotorWeek Online, Motorist Assurance Program,
PNC Bank, SafeTNet, Toyota, and Trader Online.

Library of Congress Cataloging-in-Publication Data
    Raisglid, Ron.
        Buying and leasing cars on the Internet / Ron Raisglid with
    William Mikulak and Cheri Turner.
          p. cm.
        Includes index.
        ISBN 1-58063-030-8 (alk. paper)
        1. Automobiles—Purchasing—Computer network resources.
    2. Automobile leasing and renting—Computer network resources.
    3. Electronic commerce. 4. Internet (Computer network)—Directories.
    I. Mikulak, William. II. Turner, Cheri. III. Title.
    TL162.R35 1998
    629.222'029'6—dc21   98-39328
                                                 CIP

10 9 8 7 6 5 4 3 2 1
Design by Gary Hespenheide
Manufactured in the United States
Distributed by St. Martin's Press
First Edition

To my family—Dad and Mom, whose wisdom I have grown to admire and respect, and who helped me develop my special talents and hone my insights into human nature; and to my sister Peggy, whose encouragement and enthusiasm made this book possible.

Acknowledgments

Writing this book was really a fantasy come true. I knew the first time I set my fingers to computer keyboard that many people would be relieved to find an easy-to-use guide that made car buying fun and satisfying. For helping to make this book a reality, I would like to thank everyone at Renaissance Books, especially my editor Brenda Scott Royce. Most of all I would like to thank Cheri Turner for coming up with the idea for writing this book in the first place and asking me to be her partner on it, and Bill Mikulak for meticulously editing it. Thanks also to Pastor Don Yarborough, who has imparted to me the wisdom of scriptures, which changed my life forever, and to God for making all things possible.

Contents

Introduction

"Volkswagen: Drivers Wanted" . . . MTV-style jumpy edits and jangling music . . . Mountain ranges and serpentine roads at dusk . . . Sleek contours reflect the glinting sun . . . Steel and rubber morphs into a leaping cougar . . . Pavement bursts into flame as a Mazda blazes through the desert . . . "Financing as low as 4.9%" . . . "We'll pay off your trade no matter how much you owe!"

Everywhere you turn, you are bombarded by advertising designed to fill you with longing for the promoted vehicle, which promises to redefine you as a sexier, more successful person. Harried at work? Take to the open road and watch the heads turn as you streak by. Alone at night? A sports car will transform you into a virile sexual magnet. The automotive industry has been trying for decades to make you salivate like a Pavlovian dog over these images in hopes that you will be seized by an irresistible urge to buy their cars.

 The trickery escalates when you step into the showroom, where the prevailing method of selling vehicles involves mind games, manipulation, and downright lies. The selling game is designed to spin you from one salesperson to the next until your senses are so overloaded you'll sign anything they put in front of you just to escape. Complicated contractual language hides excess fees and convoluted mathematical sleights-of-hand wrench ever more cash from your wallet.

During my years in the automotive sales business I witnessed first-hand the duplicity conventional car sellers inflict on consumers, whom they privately refer to insultingly as *ups, mooches,* or *lay downs.* I am not proud to admit that I was part of this corrosive system for ten years. I acquired more than my share of accolades: plaques, ribbons, gold watches, and vacations as awards for being named "Salesman of the Month" and "Salesman of the Year." I once broke the company record by selling thirty-eight cars in a single month! I aggressively slam-dunked one sale after another in a never-ending game of one-upmanship against my fellow salespeople. During this time I learned how to practice all the deceptions of the business in order to meet brutal sales quotas. But as I matured and examined my life's purpose, what was once a visceral thrill became a heavy burden.

That changed in 1995, when I discovered the Internet. I realized that even in its infancy, the World Wide Web could level the playing field for all types of commerce. Its integration of text and graphics into an easy-to-use interface made an exciting new venue in which vendors could ply their trade. My natural fascination for computers combined with my extensive background in retail car sales led me to start my own company. My goal, though admittedly audacious, was simple: to transform the auto industry.

For the next two years I was ridiculed for predicting that the Internet would revolutionize the auto industry. But I was not alone in this belief. People took notice when a tiny upstart Internet auto broker, Auto-By-Tel, aired a thirty-second commercial during the Super Bowl XXX telecast in 1997. The first Internet ad to be seen on national television, the Auto-By-Tel spot sent shock waves through the auto industry because it offered an exciting alternative to the traditional way of doing business.

In the last few years, the World Wide Web has become more and more sophisticated as new capabilities have been added to incorporate sound, motion pictures, animation, and 3-D virtual reality into Web sites. But more important than the technical wizardry the Web has spawned is the new marketplace it has brought about. Success stories such as the mammoth Web bookseller Amazon.com are proof that more and more consumers find Internet commerce to be a convenient and viable alternative to traditional shopping. You can buy virtually anything online nowadays—books, CDs, flowers, stocks, and yes, even cars. The Internet provides a means for you to get the facts and cut through the hyperbole, high-gloss photography, and empty promises of traditional car sellers. It allows you to separate fact from fiction to make informed choices.

This is not the first book to expose the manipulative tricks of the automotive retail industry. Many useful books have addressed that subject thoroughly, but they are limited to combating conventional sales techniques by taking on the salespeople on their own turf—in the showroom. Those books teach you to be a ruthless negotiator, to fight for every last penny, to give as well as you get. That's hardly a satisfactory course of action for all people. For those who do not seek the thrill of battle but merely want a fair deal without hassle, the Internet provides the answer.

 To make the best use of the Internet, you need a trustworthy guide to lead you. This book is that guide. With over 22,000 World Wide Web sites pertaining to automotive issues, the Internet delivers a dazzling but confusing array of services. I approached the Net with an ingrained skepticism that I developed during my years in conventional automotive sales. Yet I found it to be a remarkable alternative to this highly evolved system of manipulation. New Internet businesses are determined to compete based on price, not hype.

True, some manufacturers fill their Web sites with the same glitzy advertising that they use in mainstream media, and some traditional dealerships merely extend their promotional overkill to the Web. But they face an onslaught from businesses intent on undercutting their prices while providing more reliable information upon which to base a buying decision. Every transaction that once required you to endure high-pressure salespeople and mathematical shenanigans is now available stress-free on the Internet. Without making any commitments, you can gather all the information you need to perform direct comparisons of everything from auto parts to insurance rates to auto loans to warranties.

Use this book as your on-ramp to the automotive information superhighway. With my techniques as your road guide, you can set a course for the absolute lowest prices on all your automotive transactions. I will help you make sense of the burgeoning Internet marketplace to save you lots of money on your auto purchases, accessories, financing, insurance, repairs, and warranties. Once you explore some of these sites at your own pace you will find that car buying can actually be fun.

While you may be tempted to skip ahead to the chapter that covers the particular transaction you are interested in now, I urge you to read through the entire book before making a purchase, as other chapters may provide information that will influence your decision. If you are looking to buy a new car, chapter 5 shows you the steps to take, but you should also study chapter 9 to learn about your financing options and to calculate exactly what you can afford. Maybe you'll discover that your budget is better suited to buying a used car. In that case, turn to chapter 6. And if you've got a trade-in, chapter 8 will show you how little effort it takes to make more money by selling it yourself. If you haven't decided whether to buy or lease, chapter 7 will teach you how to compare the costs and benefits of each using handy calculators found on the Internet. And before transmitting any of your personal information over the Internet, you'll want to read about security issues discussed in chapter 4.

You might think that chapter 10 on insurance and chapter 11 on repairs will only be relevant after you've purchased your car. But reading these before you buy will help you make your decision. They show you how to avoid lemons as well as vehicles that cost a lot to maintain or insure.

Chapter 12 takes you through the easiest ways you can connect to the Internet. It is especially useful to the neophyte, showing that you don't even have to own a computer to make great use of this book. Chapter 14 provides a comprehensive guide to the best Web sites I've found, divided into common-sense categories for your convenience. Throughout the book you will encounter computer- or automotive-related terms in *italics*. These terms are concisely defined in the glossary at the back of the book.

Fasten your cyberbelts. We are about to embark on an adventure that will change your automotive buying habits forever.

Chapter One

How the Internet Saves You Thousands on Car Purchases

"Private information is
practically the source of every
large modern fortune."
—Oscar Wilde

Americans purchase approximately 60 million cars annually, primarily by haggling for hours in showrooms full of high-pressure salespeople. The currently available books and pamphlets teach the car buyer how to counter the various tricks dealerships use in order to beat them at the art of negotiation. But do you have to develop a sharklike personality and engage in psychological warfare in order to get a good deal on your next automotive purchase? Not anymore.

The alternative is the Internet. The Internet provides anyone access to information, facts, and figures that were once the closely guarded secrets of the industry. With this information literally at your fingertips, you can get the best possible deal on a new or used vehicle regardless of your age, race, gender, or social class. The Internet is home to a new breed of automotive business that is willing to bypass the manipulative emotional appeals integral to showroom sales tactics. These businesses' Web sites give consumers the resources to comparison shop and unravel the mysteries of automotive transactions from the comfort of their own homes. Without a predatory sales force circling for the kill, Internet users can conduct automotive business at their leisure. Dealerships that resist the Internet may soon find themselves at such a competitive disadvantage they will sink into oblivion.

The Internet can even simulate the showroom experience of visually examining the vehicles you're considering. Some car manufacturers' Web sites create a virtual showroom using *photo bubble* technology, which provides a 360-degree panoramic view of cars for sale. You can study every detail of the car of your dreams inside and out before you set foot in a dealership. Then you can go to the car lot for a test drive.

 But what if you don't have a "souped-up" computer with an Internet connection? Inexpensive television set-top boxes (such as WebTV), sold at most home electronics stores, are bringing the Internet to homes without computers. Internet-capable personal computers are readily available for under $1,000. Schools, libraries, and cyber-cafés offer Internet-connected computers to the public for free or for a nominal charge. Many public libraries host sessions on how to access the Internet from library computers. There is no need for this technology to pass you by even if you do not own a computer, as you will learn in chapter 12.

Once you have your Internet connection, where do you begin? By a recent count there are more than 22,000 Web sites dedicated to the automotive industry. These Web sites include dealers, manufacturers, financing and leasing companies, insurers, car clubs, auto magazines, and information services. Nearly every major automaker, dealership, and related auto industry provider has set up shop in cyberspace. Finding reputable sites that suit your needs can be an exercise in frustration. The amount of information available on the Web is so overwhelming that many people give up because they don't know where to look.

This book helps untangle the Web by identifying the best sites for every aspect of the automotive industry, leading you step-by-step through several examples. By following the simple steps outlined in this book, you will discover what the true costs are for any vehicle so you won't ever again be fooled by the sticker price. You will be able to avoid dealer doubletalk and prejudicial pricing practices. Best of all, you will save hundreds, or possibly thousands, of dollars on automotive purchases, leases, parts, and repairs—and have fun doing it!

THE INTERNET FIGHTS "BUSINESS AS USUAL"

Car dealers have developed their intimidating sales techniques over decades. Despite the tireless efforts of such consumer advocates as Ralph Nader, much of what goes on inside dealerships is con artistry of the highest order. But the Internet offers consumers both an education and an alternative to what used to be the only showroom in town. The established dealerships must now face real competition from Internet sellers intent on providing great value without the hard sell.

Dave Illingworth, a senior vice president of Toyota, USA, predicted recently that the shift to Internet-based sales will "hit the automotive industry like a tsunami" with a force that will either destroy car dealerships or lead them to new heights of success. The dealers who won't survive are the ones who refuse to take this new technology seriously and scoff at selling their cars to Internet geeks. But if dealerships do not prepare themselves for the auto buyers' revolution, they will not stay in business. According to *Time* magazine, as of May 1998 an estimated 15 percent of all new car buyers consult the Internet in making their purchase. Illingworth predicts "in conservative figures" that within the next three years, 40 percent of all car sales will be accomplished through the Internet. Consulting firm J. D. Power & Associates puts that number at 50 percent in two years.

 A 1998 J. D. Power survey also found that 48 percent of car dealers view the Internet as a threat. Bill Vann, owner of a Ford dealership affiliated with Autobytel.com Inc., is one of the growing number of dealers who has embraced Internet sales. He told *Road & Track*, "Buyers who use the Internet are shrewd and educated. They force you to lay out all your cards." Though his dealership's per-unit profit margin is narrower for cars sold over the Internet, Vann says his dealership is selling more than eight times its expected volume due to his affiliation with Autobytel.com.

Although the Internet auto industry is in its infancy, this book reveals how thoroughly it is already transforming the business by putting the consumer in control of the facts. Here is but one example of information that is now available thanks to the Internet.

THE ORIGINAL MANUFACTURER'S INVOICE

The essence of a car dealership is not the building, its hardworking staff, or even its cars. Without question the most highly guarded secret of the dealership is the book of its *manufacturer's invoices,* showing what the dealers actually paid for their cars. Until the Internet made invoices available to the public, the only people who could review the real dealership purchase price were the owner, the sales managers, and a few of the *corporate representatives*. Salespeople working the field for over twenty years would never get to see what a real invoice looked like, and if they did, they'd be subject to immediate termination.

This industry-wide secrecy lasted for many years because sales managers made plenty of money on customers who bought during the initial showroom visit. They could afford to abandon the comparison shoppers who demanded to see invoices. This code of silence worked as long as every dealer played along, so that all of them benefited. Rather than compete against each other by cutting profits, dealers would offer add-ons like undercoating and acrylic wax "at no extra charge" to keep a customer from bolting to another dealer. But customers who insisted on a written quote were out of luck. The dealership assumed they would be lost to the competition anyway, so it wasn't worth wasting time on them.

This game played out successfully for decades because it was the only game in town. Furthermore the dealerships realized how to hold customers captive with elaborate strategies involving several sales-people over the course of four to six hours. After spending that much time in the showroom, few buyers were willing to pick up shop and move to another dealership to endure the same grind all over again. Behind it all, the dealer invoices were the trump cards kept hidden from view. A dealership would sooner let a customer walk and lose a deal than let anyone look at an invoice.

 The Internet pulls these trump cards out of the dealers' sleeves and places them on the table for consumers to examine. You will save thousands of dollars on car purchases because you can see what the car and its various options actually cost dealers. This immediately levels the playing field by giving you the same information wielded by the professionals.

This book will take you to Web sites that list the manufacturer's invoices on the vehicles you desire. This enables you to compare the *manufacturer's suggested retail price* (MSRP), also called *sticker price* and *list price,* to the *manufacturer's invoice price* (MIP)—what the car actually cost the dealership. This information is crucial in determining what the dealer's bottom-line asking price is because in most cases, this bottom line is usually just $100 over the manufacturer's invoice. In a growing number of cases, dealers may even be willing to sell at *invoice.* That price can be thousands of dollars less than the sticker price.

How can dealerships afford to sell cars at such a slim profit margin? Their real cost is less than the invoice price. Automobile manufacturers give dealerships *kickbacks* or *holdbacks* that range from 3 to 4 percent of the MSRP of the vehicle. On many occasions I have seen dealerships sell cars at the invoice price and still make a substantial profit just on these kickbacks alone.

OTHER INFORMATION THE INTERNET GIVES YOU

The Internet saves you money because it shows you where to get not only the lowest new and used vehicle prices but also the lowest prices on accessories, service, insurance, and financing. It can direct you to late-breaking news items about your vehicle of choice and provide consumer advice and safety information. Within a few short minutes you will be able to discover the value of your trade-in, what your vehicle should cost, and what your monthly payments will be. You can go to Internet auto broker sites that will solicit participating dealerships to competitively bid to sell you the exact vehicle of your choice, including only those options you select. You can use the Internet to actually make the contract with a dealership, finance the purchase, have the car washed and prepped, and, in many cases, delivered to your door.

If you have been buying cars by engaging in nerve-wracking negotiations the old-fashioned way, you may be shocked when the following chapters show you how much you overspent. But now you will have the facts at your disposal and you will never be hoodwinked again. No longer will fast-talking hucksters daunt you. You will know how to set the terms of the deal you want and walk away from any salesperson who'd rather play mind games. Buying a car will become more fun than you ever imagined!

Using the Internet you can buy a car for $100 over the manufacturer's invoice price (MIP), which can be hundreds or thousands below manufacturer's suggested retail price (MSRP).

Chapter Two

Revolution in the Auto Industry: The Death of a Salesman

"For a salesman there is no rock
bottom to the life."
—Arthur Miller

A while back I attended one of the regular sales meetings held at a very large car dealership. Each of these presentations focuses on a main theme to motivate the sales staff. The topic for that Monday morning was "gaining control of the customer." Someone asked, "What happens when a customer walks in and just asks for the bottom line on a car without taking a test drive or filling out a credit application?"

The seasoned sales manager responded, "Well, you take him into your office and sell him on the dealership. Explain to him that we sell so many cars because our prices are low and we give award-winning service. Ask him about his needs and be a good listener. Start to build a relationship of trust. Then get him to take a test drive. If you give the customer numbers up front you will lose him to another dealership as a comparison shopper. It's very important for the customer to become so emotionally attached to the car he will negotiate a deal and drive off in the car that same day. 'Mr. Customer,' you say, 'I will give you all the information you want—the monthly payment, the down payment, the trade-in allowance if you have a trade—but first let's make sure this is the right car for you. Is that fair?'"

This presentation does sound fair. But it doesn't give the customer what he asked for, which is the bottom-line price. Instead it intoxicates him with new car sensations—sleek exterior paint and chrome, fine upholstery, richly appointed fixtures—while cementing his friendship with the salesperson. And who wants to disappoint new friends?

The meeting continued until the resident sales superstar got up and asked, "And what do you do when some Internet geek comes into the dealership with his printout of an Edmund's vehicle invoice report? He knows exactly what he wants and he has the invoice price of the car. On top of that he wants half the holdback. I had one guy who knew what cars were about to be shipped to us and *I don't even have access to that information.* What's up with that, boss?"

Everyone was waiting for instructions on how to defuse this ticking bomb. What magic spell could salespeople cast over Internet-educated consumers to soften them into accepting high prices? The sales manager stared blankly. "Not a problem," he retorted. "You take him into your office and sell him on the dealership. . . ." He had no other recipe from his sales cookbook. I snickered silently to myself as others in the audience mumbled derogatory side comments.

The truth is, *there is no magic spell* that automotive salespeople can use to outmaneuver the informed consumer. When confronted with customers wielding Internet invoices, the smart dealership expedites its deals and rolls Net customers out so quickly they don't have a chance to interact with the high-profit conventional sales customers. But the number of Internet-savvy consumers is expanding rapidly and the deceitful sales tactics of the past will not withstand their onslaught. These customers are demanding and getting sales service centered on full disclosure of the facts and figures.

The revolution brought on by the Internet will reduce automotive prices as dealers cut back on overhead such as advertising, excessively high labor costs, and gimmicky promotions. The bloated pay for sales staff greatly contributes to overhead. The auto industry's conventional salespeople have been accustomed to annual salaries ranging from $50,000 to $175,000. *General managers* cuddle comfortably with their spouses on paychecks that frequently exceed $18,000 a month! Their high income adds dearly to the cost of the vehicles they sell.

 And how do they earn this bounty? Not by having great stores of knowledge about their products. Not by gaining customer loyalty with forthright honesty. Instead it is by perfecting the narrow specialty of bamboozling customers into paying high grosses for cars. A conventional salesperson's success is measured by how well he can convince customers that he has what they need at a price they can't turn down.

Sales managers are more seasoned salespeople who are so adept at overcoming customer resistance that their job is to take over when the initial salesperson fails to get the job done. A sales manager can take customers poised to flee the dealership and get them to trade their cars in for half what they're worth and spend more than they dreamed of to buy a new car they don't want. *Finance managers* (also called *financial counselors*) bring in thousands more dollars by signing customers up for loans at interest rates well above prime. They also pad profits by persuading customers to buy high-profit, low-value services like protection packages, extended warranties, and security systems.

These professional pickpockets have earned their dealerships millions of dollars a year, but they add greatly to overhead. If they were prevented from using their bag of unethical sales tricks, their income would reflect that of the rest of the retail industry, where salespeople and lower level sales managers earn between $28,000 and $35,000 a year on average. And on the whole, the rest of the retail industry is better versed in the products and services they sell.

 I shopped at numerous car dealerships to see if salespeople could accurately answer simple questions concerning the cars, trucks, or utility vehicles they sell. Most were hard pressed to explain horsepower, the braking system, or the advantages of their vehicles over the competition. Rather than admit ignorance, some made up answers to my questions. Just to catch up to other segments of the retail industry, automotive salespeople must learn common courtesy, study their own product line, and develop computer skills.

The automotive salespeople who are liaisons to Internet customers have begun this transformation. Knowledgeable consumers are asking tough questions that force this new breed of seller to become more educated about their vehicles. No longer can salespeople inflate their prices when customers have the real numbers at their disposal.

The keynote speaker at an automotive sales conference I attended argued that because of the Internet's penetration into the market, high gross profits on auto sales are quickly coming to an end: "Now you have to establish client loyalty by selling the dealership's reputation through testimonials from satisfied customers. You must demonstrate the quality of your service department." As I scanned the room I could tell that these words were falling on deaf ears. As long as there are still customers whose ignorance leads them to shell out thousands of extra dollars for their vehicles, these salespeople felt secure in their old ways. But their time is running out.

The Internet has exploded on the scene at a time when both the public and many industry members are fed up with the old ways of selling cars. Conventional auto salespeople have earned a reputation as predatory price gougers, streetwise but ignorant about their own products. It is no wonder that many dealership owners I interviewed chafe at their industry's notoriety and the high overhead of the current system. Although they spend little time on the sales floor, word of customer dissatisfaction reaches them. They make up for what ill will the sales staff generates with saturation advertising, paying up to tens of thousands of dollars a week for local newspaper and radio promotions.

These owners realize that their profits will greatly increase when the present conventional car sales system is put to rest. Some greet the Internet revolution with open arms as a solution to their current cost and image problems. As the Internet supplants their conventional customer base, they will be able to cut the size of their sales staff and winnow down salaries. They can also slash advertising costs, and best of all, they can forge a new reputation of excellent service to replace the industry's current tarnished image.

Public relations nightmares affect not only the dealerships, but also the manufacturers they represent. Chrysler's executive vice president for sales and marketing criticized the company's franchised dealerships after a customer in Milwaukee contracted to buy a new Dodge Viper, Chrysler's limited-production sports car, and the dealership tried to renege on the deal. The *Wall Street Journal* reported that when the car arrived, the dealership sued the customer to get out of the contract because the dealership believed that it could sell the car for as much as $20,000 over the sticker price. This prompted the vice president to blast the system, asserting, "We have to change the entire culture of our franchises."

Some are making changes already. As the Internet forces dealerships to compete on the basis of price, they may soon whittle their profit margins down so low that cars will routinely be sold *under* invoice. They will make all of their money on the manufacturer's *holdback,* while streamlining costs enough to maintain strong profits. At an industry convention this year, I spoke with a regional director of Ford Motor Company and was surprised to learn that Ford has been considering the possibility of selling new cars at megastores like Wal-Mart.

This will certainly be a major cultural change for the conventional auto sales industry and it marks a great victory for consumers by applying the same price competition to cars that has made other merchandise more affordable.

The revolution in the auto industry follows on the heels of revolutions in other retail industries. Home electronics went through a price and labor metamorphosis six years ago. There was a time in that industry when good salespeople made $75,000 a year by manipulating and arm-twisting their customers. Today electronics salespeople are much more customer-centered and knowledgeable. Customers no longer face high-pressure sales tactics when shopping for stereo systems in retail stores, from catalogs, or, of course, on the Internet.

The major-appliance industry is another good example of this trend. Economic pressure forced sales staff salaries in places like Sears down from the late 1980s peak that topped $80,000 annually to an average of $35,000 today. Cutting labor costs allows retailers to sell washing machines and refrigerators at significantly lower prices. The auto industry is about to follow in the footsteps of the home appliance and home electronics industries, if it can overcome some viciously ingrained discriminatory practices.

PRICE DISCRIMINATION AGAINST WOMEN AND MINORITIES

Pricing of major appliances and home electronics is standardized. Women and minorities pay the same prices for refrigerators or stereo receivers as white males. Sale prices apply equally to all who enter the store, whether they are male, female, white, black, Asian, or Hispanic. Wouldn't it be nice if the same rules applied to car buying? Unfortunately, laws against sexual and racial discrimination have not been well enforced in the automotive retail industry.

There is a major distinction between the way automotive manufacturers and the manufacturers' franchised dealerships treat their customers. Manufacturers realize that women are involved in 53 percent of all automotive decisions and that they purchase over a third of all light trucks made in the United States. Three out of four women between the ages of twenty and fifty-five are in the work force, so it is no surprise that auto manufacturers covet this segment of the market.

The manufacturers have wisely responded by researching women's automotive needs and designing such model lines as the Toyota Celica, Acura Integra, Volkswagen Cabrio, Ford Explorer, Dodge Caravan, and Mitsubishi Eclipse.

In contrast, automotive *dealerships* are less interested in serving their female and minority clients. Often car salespeople judge customers by their sex, race, and class when deciding who is vulnerable enough to accept grossly inflated price quotes. Many females and minorities who have suspected that they are treated worse than their white male counterparts have good reason to feel that way. There is solid evidence to corroborate their suspicions.

Ian Ayres, a professor at Stanford Law School and a research fellow of the American Bar Association, conducted a three-year test of how well competitive market forces eliminate price discrimination based on race and gender. He looked at the retail automobile industry as "particularly ripe for scrutiny." The results were published as the lead article in the *Harvard Law Review* in February 1991.

The study employed white men, white women, black men, and black women as testers who posed as prospective customers. They conducted 180 independent negotiations at 90 dealerships in the Chicago area, in which all deals were made for cash with no trade-ins involved. What Ayres found would not surprise those working in the industry nor would it shock female and minority customers who have believed themselves to be subject to discriminatory treatment.

The dealerships gave the white males the best deals, while the deals they offered the white women included a profit margin that was 40 percent higher on average. Deals for the black males included a profit margin 100 percent higher than their white counterparts, and deals for the black females included a profit margin 200 percent higher.

Ayres also demonstrated that the testers were directed to sales members of their own gender and race. This practice is commonly used because people of similar backgrounds tend to trust each other more and are thus willing to pay more. The conventional car sales industry has made discriminatory sales practices a science.

Ayres offers several contributing factors to explain the study's results:

1. Dealerships are permitted to charge different amounts to different people for the exact same vehicle.

2. The less competition there is between dealerships for a given sale, the more profit the dealership is likely to make.

3. The dealership assumes that prospects will avoid comparison shopping because they are uninformed about the dynamics of automotive sales, they don't have the time to shop, or they just dislike the shopping experience and want to complete the task as fast as they can.

4. Societal stereotypes based on gender or race encourage salespeople to offer sucker deals to female and minority customers. They are seen as *lay downs,* customers who "lay down" rather than resist huge markups.

A larger test of four hundred additional negotiations in the Chicago area supported the results of this initial study. In my own experience, such discrimination continues today among conventional car dealers. *Black Enterprise* confirmed this state of affairs in its April 1997 article "Are You Being Taken for a Ride?", which showed that blacks are charged more than whites for new and used automobiles. It advised car shoppers to avoid high-pressure sales tactics and consider using the Internet to buy a car.

THE INTERNET HELPS OVERCOME DISCRIMINATION

The government's antidiscrimination laws are notoriously difficult to enforce because people make subjective judgments about each other all the time in the course of doing business. Clear, consistent patterns of discrimination take a long time to recognize and quantify, as Ian Ayres's study shows. But now the Internet acts as an equalizer for those seeking a level playing field when shopping for automobiles.

 When you use the Internet, you may be struck by how easy it is to maintain your anonymity. No one sees you or hears your voice as you click your mouse and type at the keyboard. You can obtain the same information from various Internet sources whatever your gender, race, sexual preference, age, income, or disability. Even those who cannot afford a personal computer have ample opportunity to learn how to surf the Net at their local libraries, universities, and cyber-cafés. This means that anyone can go into a dealership carrying a printout from the Internet of the manufacturer's invoice for their chosen vehicle and ask to pay at most $100 over that cost.

Once a dealership's sales staff discovers that you know their costs and profits, they often acknowledge that their game is over. They know that if they don't make the deal you seek, a competitor will. Salespeople are no longer in control of pricing. You have the numbers, the ability, and the willingness to walk out. They cannot easily dismiss you as, say, a stereotypically ditzy woman befuddled by automotive jargon. They are forced to see an informed person who can negotiate competently. The best they can do is to usher you in and out of the contracting room quickly to keep you from talking to other customers.

No matter who you are, by using the Internet you will know the actual cost of the car (see chapter 5), the value of your trade-in (see chapter 8), and the lowest interest rates available for purchase (see chapter 9) or lease (see chapter 7). All the cards will be on the table so dealerships no longer have unfair advantage over you. The Internet has revolutionized the auto industry by making formerly secret information accessible to all. The car dealers who agree to play by the new rules will rehabilitate their reputations from shameless hucksters to pillars of integrity.

BACKLASH!

This rehabilitation may be a slow and painful process because some salespeople will cling to old ways and the new breed of honorable dealers will suffer from residual resentment that customers have harbored against them for decades. Results from a recent customer satisfaction survey reveal quite a disparity between how consumers feel about their car manufacturers and how they feel about their dealerships. For example, in 1997 Toyota customers ranked Toyota dealerships second from the bottom in satisfaction while expressing great love for their cars. This happened despite the fact that Toyota dealerships engaged in survey data-tampering by asking customers to bring their completed surveys back to the dealership rather than send them directly to the manufacturer. In exchange the dealerships gave customers free oil changes or discounts on other services. That way they could select only the most favorable survey responses to send in.

But even dealerships that behaved admirably toward their Internet customers received low ratings. Customers who use the Internet rank their satisfaction with dealerships lower than customers who do not use the Internet, despite the fact that Internet customers can now walk into a dealership, get the best deal possible and be out in record time.

How do we explain why Internet customers give their dealerships poor scores across the board? I believe it's a backlash against the industry now that the Internet has revealed the deceptive practices and huge profit margins dealers have enjoyed all these years. It's no wonder that customers feel betrayed by past abuse and continue to hold dealerships in contempt.

The automotive retail industry has some tough times ahead despite the fall in car prices instigated by the Internet. But in the end we will all benefit from the widespread availability of price information.

INTERNET AUTOMOTIVE BUYING IS REALLY *FUN!*

Imagine yourself sitting on a tropical island beach located somewhere near paradise. The sky is admiral blue, the aqua water glitters in the noon sun. You sip a frosty-cold mint julep and pass the day in pure bliss and tranquillity. Covet the moment because now imagine that you are driving into a dealership's parking lot with ten hungry salespeople leering at you. You are about to enter the "Headlight Zone" and for the next six hours, you will experience unimaginable pressure, manipulation, and lies that a team of pros will employ to slam-dunk you into a new car. What a contrast!

My point in comparing these two experiences is that they have long been diametric opposites. Purchasing a car using the Internet may never be as pleasurable as relaxing on a tropical island but *it will be fun!* Let me assure some of my younger readers that there was a time, decades ago, when buying a new car was a great family affair. The entire family piled into the station wagon to go down to the dealership to pick out a new car together.

But current studies concerning our least enjoyed activities rank visiting a car dealership as the worst chore we must face, even below going to the dentist. People would rather get their teeth extracted than their money. The next chapter's tales from the land of conventional automotive dealerships illustrate why root canal is considered more pleasurable than car buying.

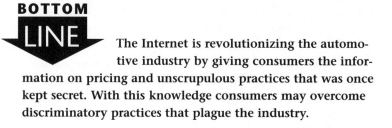 The Internet is revolutionizing the automotive industry by giving consumers the information on pricing and unscrupulous practices that was once kept secret. With this knowledge consumers may overcome discriminatory practices that plague the industry.

Chapter Three

Small Lies, Big Lies, and Dastardly Lies

"The best liar is he who makes the smallest amount of lying go the longest way."
—Samuel Butler

If you think ignorance is bliss, either you are a car seller or you acquire hand-me-down vehicles from your Uncle John. Automotive salespeople depend on your ignorance. They are not necessarily professional or knowledgeable about their product but they are well trained in the art of maximizing profit for themselves and their dealership. They are certainly not working to be your friends. If you are unfortunate to find one who has plaques and honors proudly displaying "Salesman of the Month," you must assume you are dealing with someone who knows how to size you up and skillfully separate you from your money. No matter how you feel about your salesperson, he or she is never on your side and will never try to get you a good deal.

Automotive salespeople are constantly learning new ways to transfer your cash to their coffers. They have corporate newsletters, sales meetings, training seminars, videotapes, marketing institutes, outside trainers, and motivational training courses. Tapes and videos abound to teach salespeople how to overcome your objections. In sales meetings, *you* are the enemy. Salespeople openly discuss tactics to defeat *you*, sharing notes on "problem customers" and trading secrets for closing deals. Then they go back to the showroom floor and wait for you.

When you walk into a sales department at a dealership you are quickly judged as a good customer or a bad customer, a "nice guy" or a "jerk." Nice guys want to be friends with and trust the salesperson; jerks want a good deal. Nice guys look for a salesperson's approval; jerks look in their copy of the *Edmund's Price Guide*. Nice guys agree to the first price offered; jerks stand their ground and refuse to be railroaded. Nice guys drive away in an overpriced car after their initial visit; jerks are not afraid to walk away from a bad deal. Jerks may even visit the dealership many times while they comparison shop.

Salespeople have the most powerful tool to convert jerks into nice guys: practice. Your interaction with car salespeople may come once every two to seven years, but in the meantime they fine tune their skills every day. The best are brilliantly streetwise, sizing up your needs, your psyche, and your ego in an instant. They use all their resources to position you to buy . . . not tomorrow or later today, but right now. And they will say just about anything to get you to say "yes."

FRONT-END VERSUS BACK-END PROFIT

Dealerships can make even more money on an array of options they get you to buy after shaking hands on the price of the car than they do on the car itself. The profit they make selling the car for a price above the manufacturer's invoice is called the *front-end* profit. While this profit can be hefty, it often pales in comparison to the possibilities of the *back-end* profit. These include *protection packages,* security systems, *maintenance contracts,* additional options and warranties, your trade if you have one, and financing and insurance. As you can imagine, each offers ample opportunity to drain your bank account.

My goal is to empower you, the consumer, to find all the information you need right at your fingertips on the Internet. Then you can develop an overall plan to cut down both their front-end and back-end profits so that you protect your wallet, defeat your enemy, and win the day!

THE TRUTH WILL SET YOU FREE

I hope by now you are convinced that buying a car should never be an impulsive purchase. Going up against a conventional sales department that has developed its underhanded and nefarious tactics over many years requires a full set of battle plans. All *sales managers* teach their staff that selling cars is a game of orchestrating your emotions; the most ethically dubious tactics of the trade result in the most money.

The saying goes, "Let the buyer beware," and I will actually teach you how to *be* aware. The following are commonly used deceptions you need to know if you wish to come out a winner. Later chapters will show you how to use the Internet to counter these tricks by arming yourself with information.

SLASH-IT SALES

You read an ad in the local newspaper proclaiming that Wheeler Dealer Motors is having a *slash-it* sale with used cars selling for as low as $99. That's not $99 down or $99 a month, that's $99 for the whole car. It sounds too good to be true but after all, it's in print, so you rationalize to yourself, "Maybe the dealership is selling *loss leaders*."

The slash-it sale is scheduled to begin at 8 A.M. Sunday morning. If you get there at 7:30 A.M., you figure you will be first in line, but surprise! There are already over three hundred people ahead of you. It's like a carnival: multicolored helium-filled balloons, a band, banners, and, of course, plenty of free refreshments for the prospective buyers.

At 8 A.M. the "fun" begins. The master of ceremonies, sporting a western-style outfit and wired with an amplifier, begins to explain the rules. Salespeople are already deftly working the crowds and screening for those willing to complete credit applications. "When the gates open at 8:30," explains the MC, "you pick the car you want and sit in it. Then I will stop by your car to slash the list price, which will be in plain view on the windshield. If by chance you leave your car for any reason while the presentation is in progress, someone else will have the right to sit in that car and obtain the ridiculously low slash-it price."

The slash-it hoax plays out like a TV game show. An entourage of cheering friends, relatives, and curious onlookers are right on the MC's heels yelling, "Slash it! Slash it!" as he walks from car to car. The MC arrives at the car that you are hoping to buy for $99. You start to hope, "Even if it's not the $99 one, maybe I can still get a great deal if he slashes it low enough."

The MC approaches your car and shouts out the list price already marked on the car. The crowd cheers, "Slash it! *Slash it!*" The MC lowers the price by $400. "Slash it! Slash it!" screams the crowd as you join in the chorus. The price is dropped another $200 and then the MC declares that the "slashing" is over.

He then challenges you to buy the car at the slashed price by stating, "We are practically giving this car away and I am going to take another $100 off the price just because you are such a great participant. Now, sir, are you ready to sign the contract and drive away in this beautiful vehicle?"

"Yes!" you scream, caught up in the hysteria, and then you are hastily escorted by a salesperson to the *F&I (finance and insurance) department,* where the DMV forms are completed, the contract is signed, and the car is prepared for delivery.

What is really going on here? This event has clearly been a well-orchestrated emotional hype. The cars are marked at list price. The dealership slashes the price by an insignificant amount. In fact, the car you selected is reduced far less than if you had just walked into the dealership any time of day and bargained your way down.

Are you shaking your head and wondering how people can be so foolish as to fall for this *obvious* scam? I am sure you would never be hoodwinked by a slash-it sale. But even you, under the right circumstances, can get caught up in this frenzy. We all share the same human frailties that dealerships have learned to artfully finesse. It is not surprising that the day after these slash-it sales, dealerships are deluged by complaints of angry people with buyer's remorse. Unfortunately, there is no cooling-off period when you buy a car.

This new fad is sweeping the nation. Dealerships are able to move 40 to 60 percent of their used car stock and especially aged stock in less than four hours with this promotion. And what about the $99 dollar used cars? Here is where the maxim "You get what you pay for" truly applies. The $99 dollar cars are usually in such poor condition that people won't purchase them at any price. After all, the ad never stated which cars would be displayed for $99 or what their condition was. Is this scam a small lie, a big lie, or a dastardly lie? You decide.

DEALER'S DISCOUNT COUPONS

Have you ever found yourself clipping a coupon to save hundreds of dollars on a car? All you have to do is bring the coupon in to the dealership. Oh, yes, by the way, this coupon must be presented to the dealership for validation *upon your arrival*. If you present this coupon *after* you've made your best deal, you can bet there isn't a tiger's chance in Hades that it will be accepted. When you present the coupon up front, the sales people have plenty of opportunity to add some hidden expense to compensate, but not after you've concluded negotiations. In fact, the discount is nonexistent, a ploy to get you into the showroom.

Why do people fall for obvious lies like this one? We want to believe in the fundamental goodness of business people. We like to feel we are lucky at spotting bargains that sound too good to be true. We hope for the best in the absence of facts. We would rather trust others than take control of the situation.

Car dealers rely on such fundamentals of human nature. I remember one dealership in particular had extraordinary success using this promotion. Fifty determined buyers came in holding their $1,000 coupons, excited about getting a great deal that, of course, would never materialize.

BAIT AND SWITCH

Bait and switch is a common tactic used by wily retailers of all types. A car is advertised for a fabulously low price, but when you enter the dealership in response to the ad, the car is unavailable. Instead the salesperson skillfully attempts to switch you to a more expensive car that you never wanted in the first place.

Not only is this practice dishonest, it's illegal. If it happens to you, report the dealership to your state's Attorney General and the Department of Motor Vehicles. This deception will become more difficult to practice as more consumers use the Internet to educate themselves about their rights as consumers.

THE SWITCH

Even in the absence of any phony bait, some salespeople will still attempt to shift your attention away from the car that first interests you. Whatever you do, do not seek their recommendation for the best car on the lot. Asking a car salesperson to recommend a car is like asking a waitress to recommend an entrée. The waitress receives her standing orders from the cook; the salesperson takes orders from another figure of authority: the bottom line. The salesperson will invariably try to point you to whatever yields the highest profit margin.

It may be that the car you were eyeing is already in negotiation with another customer. Indeed, you might have chosen a model that is flying off the lot, while the salesperson hopes to steer you toward one that isn't selling. Whatever the reason for the switch, it has more to do with the salesperson's needs than your own. If you feel yourself weakening, remember the first lesson of automobile acquisition: *No matter how you feel about your salesperson, he or she is never on your side and will never try to get you a "good deal."*

SOLD BELOW COST

In all my years of working behind the scenes at dealerships, I have only found five occasions where a car was sold below cost. The first was a salesperson's error on a written quote that the dealership was forced to honor. Then there was an ugly purple car that couldn't be given away. The other three were involved in light accidents, probably on test drives or during shipping, so the cars could not be sold as new.

Sometimes demonstration units or *unwinds* are sold below cost. An unwind is a vehicle that must be returned to a dealership within ten days of contracting because the customer listed false information on the credit application or a bank could not be found to underwrite the loan. When this happens the car can no longer be sold as new. Frequently these cars are offered as *loss leaders* in which the dealer loses money on one car in order to mislead buyers into believing that many such vehicles are available at this very low price. Of course, once in the showroom, buyers are given the switch to a higher priced vehicle.

"THERE IS NO DISCOUNT"

Statistically, one out of seven purchasers believes that the sticker price of a car is the true cost of the vehicle. This group contains the genuine suckers and is considered the dealerships' bread and butter. It is astonishing what lies car salespeople will tell about the sticker price. They will look sincerely in your eyes and say, "These new cars are never discounted. If they were last year's models, then I could give you a small discount."

The truth is that even some of the hottest selling Japanese vehicles are heavily discounted if you know how to get to the real rock-bottom price.

FRIENDS AND RELATIVES BEWARE!

You walk into the dealership smug and confident because you have a connection, a friend or relative who will give you a steal. In reality, you may be offered a modest discount, which will be touted as a "great deal" but isn't. In fact, friends and relatives put up the least resistance to high pricing and are always considered *lay downs*. Think about it: A high percentage of referrals come from family, friends, and acquaintances, so salespeople are not likely to reduce their commissions by offering each of them big bargains. It is better to purchase your car from a complete stranger because only then will you be free of guilt when pressing for the best price.

CASE STUDY: THE UNSUSPECTING SISTER

When Brenda went to buy a Dodge Colt Vista, she thought she would get a fabulous deal because she had an inside track: Her brother-in-law Dave worked at a Dodge dealership. Dave, the parts manager, passed her on to a salesman, Steve, and told her she'd be in good hands. Steve warned Brenda that the sticker price only had a tiny profit margin built in and therefore there was no room for bargaining. Brenda believed Steve because she trusted Dave and knew he wouldn't steer her wrong.

Because of this misplaced trust, not only did Brenda pay full sticker price for the car, she also financed the car through the dealership, purchased an *extended warranty,* and paid for disability insurance on the loan. It wasn't until years later, when she learned the techniques discussed in this book, that Brenda realized how foolhardy she'd been. By going to her brother-in-law's dealership, she thought she was getting a good deal with no pressure. Instead she willingly spent thousands of dollars more than she should have, giving Dave's dealership a hefty profit for virtually no work.

 There is an old saying in the car business: "Sticker is quicker." It's true, paying sticker price will get you on the road quicker but as Brenda eventually discovered, "quicker" comes at a high cost. This is an industry that routinely encourages salespeople to bilk their own friends and relatives for profit.

WEARING YOU DOWN

Dealerships train salespeople to anticipate your questions and respond with a whirlwind of numbers and a steady stream of reassurances. After several hours of grinding, your eyeballs are rolling around in their sockets. You've been given the *T.O.* by being *turned over* from one person to the next until you face the dealership's smoothest talking pro. At this point the salespeople know you will sign just about anything. Are you really going to leave this showroom to start all over in another? No way! Now they have you beat. You want the deal over and done with. Like sheep waiting to be fleeced, you too will line up to do the dealer's bidding. I witness this every day.

FREE TINTED GLASS, FREE UNDERCOATING, AND OTHER OPTIONS

There will be a minimum margin of profit below which the dealership will not go. This is their bottom line. However, by "giving away" options instead of reducing the price of the car, the salesperson maintains the wide margin. The extras look enticing, but their sticker prices are quite inflated, while the actual dealer cost for providing them is nominal. For example, a "mop and glo" is a so-called paint protector that costs the customer $400 and the dealership about $8. But the dealer hopes giving it away will be enough to keep a reluctant customer from heading off the lot.

THE LOWBALL

In this scenario you have already tried to negotiate a deal but it fell apart. Perhaps you couldn't come to a mutually agreeable figure. Maybe your salesperson wasn't able to get approval for the price you both discussed. As you are walking out the door the salesperson beckons to you and says, "I think I may be able to get the price to about what you are looking for if you can come back tomorrow." The attractive figure the salesperson throws out gets your attention. But it is a lie. This practice is called *lowballing.*

Lowballing accomplishes two objectives for the salesperson: First, it locks you into an unrealistic price and freezes you out of a deal with someone else; second, it gets you to return to the dealership. For example, Mrs. Durkins decided to do some preliminary research into the purchase of a car. She informed the salesperson that she and her husband would have to make the final decision about the purchase together but that she would like to bring the cost information about the car back home to her husband. The salesperson gave her a range of what the car could cost her and gave her a monthly payment: "Well, Mrs. Durkins, this car will run you anywhere from $280 to $370 dollars a month." The dealership could not possibly sell the car for $280 a month and knew if she tried to comparison shop the next dealership down the road will not be able to either.

If the dealer sends you off with a lowball figure, that figure will evaporate when you return. And so will your resistance, the salesperson hopes. Lowballing is intended to wear you down. It sends you home full of hope. All night long you will be thinking about how good you will look in that car and how much fun it will be to drive. You will start to make plans around owning it. The sales department knows that once you have spent several hours in their clutches they can usually manipulate you to sign the sales contract.

This method works. It is the cornerstone of all conventional sales departments. The art of eroding your resistance has been perfected over many years. When the salesperson attempts to lowball you, try to make the deal right then and there. Ask to speak with the manager and insist that you are willing to sign for the car and to make your initial payment immediately based on the lowball offer. Although it is unlikely, you may be able to pick up the car at this attractive price.

THE DEPOSIT AND THE BUMP

Salespeople use a few variations of this ploy to lighten your wallet. You might know what car you want, the model, color, options, and price, but the dealership doesn't have it on the lot. The salesperson will tell you not to worry because this exact model is being shipped and is expected in a few days. He asks you for a check to hold or a credit card number that he promises not to process. In return you get a receipt showing the model number and the price that he is offering.

Done deal? Don't count on it! You have just been duped by the *bump*. Unless the salesperson includes the VIN (vehicle identification number) on your receipt and cashes your check or processes your credit card, the dealer is under no obligation to sell you anything. Meanwhile if you gave your credit card number, your driver's license, or your social security number, the dealership probably pulled a credit report on you without asking your permission. They may have even sent loan applications on your behalf to various financing companies in anticipation of widening their profit. In fact the real purpose of asking you for a deposit is not what you believe it to be, to lock in terms you've negotiated. It's to keep you from walking out without a commitment. Now you are on the hook.

By the time you are called back in to the dealership to see your new car and sign the contract, the salesperson informs you that he will need an additional $200 for shipping, or running lights, or some other item that bumps up the price. The bump is also known as the *raise*.

The bump is also used when a *lay down* agrees to pay an elevated price too quickly. The salesperson figures that the customer can be soaked for even more money. The salesperson goes off to do the paperwork only to return and ruefully confess that the sales manager refused to accept the price he gave because it is was unfairly weighed against the dealership. But for only $400 dollars more, the sales manager *may* accept the deal. The salesperson puts on the pressure by asking, "If I can make this happen, are you willing to buy this car right now, sir?"

The way to deal with this is to refuse to give a deposit or sensitive information about yourself until you have received the manager's written acceptance of your bid on a *buyer's order*. And just as firmly reject any attempt to bump up that bid.

MOVING YOU FROM BUYING TO LEASING

This is a popular ploy that sometimes earns salespeople bonuses. You come in planning to purchase a vehicle within a pre-set budget and the salesperson convinces you that your money could actually get a much fancier model if you lease instead of buy. This increases the dealership's profit margin because (1) a lease is usually more profitable for a dealership than straight financing of a buyer's loan, and (2) a higher-priced model has more built-in profit. Even if you insist on sticking with the original model you were interested in, the dealership can make more money if you decide to lease rather than buy. Chapter 7, "To Lease or Not to Lease," shows how to decide when leasing serves you better and how to get the terms that guarantee you are the one who benefits most, not the dealership.

ADD-ONS (OPTIONS)

Fancy additions to the car's cost include such items on the dealer's sticker as *Special Value Package, Protection Package,* Striping and Special Tires, *ADP,* and *DVF.* According to Remar Sutton in *Don't Get Taken Every Time,* the special value package adds no value to your car; it is a markup that is pure profit often added to hot-selling cars. The same is true for ADP, which stands for "Additional Dealer Profit" and DVF, which means "Dealer Vacation Fund." The "special" tires are worth maybe $150 but often sell for $795. The protection package includes such things as rust-proofing, undercoating, glazing, and fabric conditioning that might only cost the dealership $150, but may be priced at $1,200. You can always get these things done to your car elsewhere for much less, but most new cars don't even need them.

Many states are adopting laws forcing manufacturers to add running lights on all their new cars. The headlights are placed on closed circuit in your car and are constantly on when you are driving. This is a good safety feature that costs the manufacturer next to nothing. However, dealerships often use this feature as an opportunity to add a few hundred dollars to the gross margin of the car, so beware. Refuse this surcharge and the dealer will almost always waive it.

Other dealer profit add-ons that you can avoid (or obtain elsewhere at a lower cost) include alarm systems, security registration, extended warranties, and maintenance contracts. You can shop around to have an alarm installed for much less than most dealerships charge and the same goes for other protection system services like security registration. Most new vehicle warranties are comprehensive enough that you don't need any other coverage. If you feel it necessary, you can shop around on the Internet for warranties (see "Warranties" in chapter 14). Never let yourself be held captive by the dealership's service charges.

 Dealerships also may strong-arm you into buying credit life or disability insurance to cover your remaining car payments in the event of an accident or loss of life. You can get much better life insurance coverage from other sources and credit disability insurance is more expensive than it is worth.

FLIPPING THE DEAL

An unwritten law among salespeople is that half a deal is better than no deal. The salesperson that first approaches you is guaranteed half of the commission of an eventual sale no matter how many salespeople you confer with afterward. Usually your first contact will be a rookie who has been on the job for less than six months. If you start resisting and your objections are not being successfully overcome, reinforcements are brought in to wear you down. When this happens you are being *flipped*.

The next in line are usually the big guns with the "Salesman of the Month" plaques proudly displayed on their walls, and their sales skills are evident as they methodically hammer away at your every objection. They try to maximize the net profit not only on a small *margin* deal that needs a boost, but also on a deal where it appears that the purchaser is an easy sell. The *easy sell* customer, affectionately known as a *pounder,* offers the potential for especially high profits. Pounders get their nicknames because they will readily accept a deal that adds a thousand dollars (one "pound") of profit to the dealership. If you think that a pounder is bad, there are plenty of two- and three-pounders out there as well.

CASE STUDY: THE UNGUARDED HEART

My good friend Chris, a veteran of automotive sales, shared an anecdote with me that illustrates how dealerships flip a deal. Ophelia, a woman in her twenties, made an appointment to test-drive the car of her dreams, a white Mustang. She was exceedingly trusting and youthfully naïve and Chris could tell right away that she was a *lay down.*

Chris saw dollar signs everywhere. He told her that she reminded him of his beloved sister and that he would take special care of her. Ophelia had a good job and established credit. However, Chris cautioned that because she was a first-time car buyer it was going to be tough making this deal work.

He eased her into the driver's seat and let her soak up the Mustang's sleek contours. Ophelia swooned during the test drive and Chris recognized that this was love at first sight. Giving her a worried look, he said, "I will try my best to get this car for you, but I need to know now if you can afford a $516 car payment for sixty months?"

She eagerly responded, "No problem!"

When she agreed to that figure, she acquiesced to a $4,000 markup from the manufacturer's invoice, an enormous front-end profit. In addition, the payments included a whopping $2,500 in financing charges, a bountiful beginning to back-end profits. It was time for Chris to flip Ophelia over to the next angler to reel this big fish in.

He left her in a comfortable office overlooking the dealership, where she could gaze longingly at her magnificent car. Upon hearing of the catch Chris hauled in, the sales manager requested of the finance manager, "Take your time with this one, nice and easy. I want every nickel we can get." The *finance manager* took over the sale, piling on warranties, security systems, and insurance to the tune of another $2,500. As Ophelia agreed to each new charge, she became an instant celebrity among the staff, who all came out to witness a real live "nine-pounder" get hauled in.

The size of this profit margin may be extreme, but Ophelia exhibited a blithe ignorance that is all too common among car buyers. Had Ophelia read this book and followed its stipulations, she would have saved thousands. Instead she was saddled with such huge payments she was forced to sell the car back to the dealership still owing more than it was worth. When this happens a customer is said to be *in the bucket* or *upside down.*

LET'S GET REAL

My intention in writing this chapter is not to make you bitter toward automotive salespeople or to the industry as a whole. Instead I want you to use my Internet-based principles to purchase your next car at the lowest possible price *and* keep your sense of humor while doing it. By the time you are finished reading this book you will be in complete control of your purchase and you will enjoy the last laugh.

Many of the principles and insights that I am about to disclose are secrets well guarded by the industry. Like the ancient Greek intellectual Diogenes, I searched the land for truth. I examined books, magazines, television, radio, consumer organizations, and public forums looking for information to counter the misleading conventional sales practices in the automotive industry. I found nothing so useful as what exists on the Internet. This new medium has become home to automobile businesses that offer a true alternative to haggling with car dealerships. They compete so effectively with the conventional sellers because they provide a humane and comfortable way of purchasing a car based on the honest disclosure of actual costs. Rest assured, my dear readers, you are at the forefront of a new era in automotive sales that will eventually strengthen the industry.

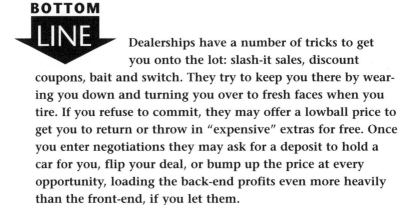

BOTTOM LINE Dealerships have a number of tricks to get you onto the lot: slash-it sales, discount coupons, bait and switch. They try to keep you there by wearing you down and turning you over to fresh faces when you tire. If you refuse to commit, they may offer a lowball price to get you to return or throw in "expensive" extras for free. Once you enter negotiations they may ask for a deposit to hold a car for you, flip your deal, or bump up the price at every opportunity, loading the back-end profits even more heavily than the front-end, if you let them.

Chapter Four

A Wide World of
Wheels in Cyberspace

"Man is still the most extraordinary computer of all."
—John F. Kennedy

Maybe today's the day you plan to begin your quest for a shining new sports coupe to replace that dilapidated heap you're ashamed to be seen in. Or perhaps you look forward to sitting higher in the saddle than you can in your Lexus sedan and you are thinking about a sports utility vehicle. It could be that a Harley-Davidson is just the thing to get your blood circulating now that you've retired. Whatever your situation, the Internet is the place to start your search.

What makes the Internet better than any other single source of automotive information? Here are just a few examples. Perhaps you saw a great commercial for the Subaru Impreza and you remember glancing at a review of it in *Car and Driver,* but in which issue? Is it one of the ones lying in a puddle of antifreeze on your garage floor? Not to worry; you can go to the magazine's Web site (**www.caranddriver.com**) and search for that review and any others that strike your fancy (see figure 4.1). Prices and other information are updated much more frequently on the Web than they can be in any print publication.

Say you're about to hop in your moldering rust-bucket to check out the used cars available along your local automotive dealers' row. But suddenly the skies open up and the streets flood from a torrential downpour. You can still make the rounds in cyberspace without suffering so much as one drop of rain. Compared to the time it takes to haul yourself from one dealership to another, *surfing the Net* is a breeze. With a click of a mouse you can move from one Web site to the next,

Figure 4.1 Car and Driver *Magazine Online*

backtrack to somewhere you've been, or stop your search in time for a rerun of *The Simpsons*. Just try to get out of a dealership as quickly once you've been dragooned by an eager salesperson.

How many dealerships are in direct competition for your money in your locality? A sad fact of the automotive sales industry is that it is consolidating. National chains are taking over many dealerships and local companies often own a number of dealerships in a region, offering multiple car lines but very little in the way of competitive pricing. In some towns, a single company owns all of the dealerships. Where can you turn for true comparison shopping? Answer: The Internet.

And here is the kicker. You retain control as you gain access to meaningful information—wholesale versus retail prices, interest rates, actual costs of options, insurance quotes, warranty terms—to help you make side-by-side comparisons of vehicles and services offered. And these are quotes that you can print out and keep for your records, not sweet lies spewed out by a cunning salesperson who refuses to commit anything to paper.

Dealerships want you to be one-stop shoppers: come on the lot, find the car you like, trade in your old car, accept their warranties, insurance, and financing. But each of these aspects of the deal is a separate consideration that requires your pre-planning and comparison-shopping.

Before you trade in your car, shouldn't you know what it's actually worth? In fact, you can usually get more for it by selling it yourself than trading it in (see chapter 8). And you definitely should decide whether to buy or lease ahead of time (see chapter 7). If you choose to buy, then financing is another realm you should check out thoroughly before going into a dealership (see chapter 9). You will get much better loan rates from a credit union or bank unaffiliated with the dealership than from one that is paying a commission to the dealer or from a manufacturer's financing company. When you have your loan secured, you can pay cash to the dealership and avoid a big chunk of their profit taking.

Because you can research all of these areas on the Internet, it offers true one-stop shopping or at least one-stop researching, you can readily compare what each company in each area of the automotive business charges without making a commitment to any of them. You don't have to look a single salesperson in the eye until you're ready.

 Let's take a brief sightseeing tour. Later chapters will guide you step-by-step through various Web sites covering all aspects of the automotive industry. Right now we'll confine our tour to a few highlights to whet your appetite for what awaits you in cyberspace. For those of you who are not yet connected to the Internet, please see chapter 12, "Internet Basics," to find out how to do so cheaply. For the rest of you, before you fire up that *browser* there are a few caveats about protecting yourself while you "surf the Net."

SAFE SURFS

You may be a seasoned Internet pro with the latest Web browser, a lightning fast connection, and a top-of-the-line computer. Or you might be poring over this book while sitting at the public library's Internet-connected computer, fearful of pushing the one wrong button that will electronically drain your life's savings into some cyber-crook's account. To ease your mind, you should realize that no one can take your money unless you input the information that allows them to do so.

So what are the real threats to your pocketbook and peace of mind on the Internet and what can be discounted as overblown figments of the media's paranoid sensationalism? In general, outright fraud is much less prevalent than subtle misrepresentation, whereas invasion of privacy occurs more frequently than you might think.

 The Internet is not immune to fraudulent business schemers. In fact, it is especially tempting to scam artists precisely because of its low entry cost and the ease of instantly *spamming,* or flooding thousands of recipients' e-mail boxes with advertising. But most of these scams are merely familiar ploys transferred to the Internet: pyramid schemes, shady investments, credit repair services, and offers of goods, services, or wealth too good to be true.

On the other hand, there are plenty of reputable businesses that have made their home on the Web. Many of the automotive sites I will discuss are online extensions of companies that have done business with the public for years. You should expect the same quality of service, timely shipment of products, and responsible handling of your credit information that you would if you placed an order with them by mail or telephone.

If you are dealing with a company you have never heard of or have questions about, you can check whether a consumer watchdog site, like Cybercop Precinct House (**www.cybercops.org**) or the Federal Trade Commission (**www.ftc.gov**), has logged any complaints against it before you place an online order.

You may also be worried that people other than the intended recipient might gain access to your credit information if you place an order online. This is no trivial concern. Credit fraud and theft of identity are increasing as criminals learn high tech methods to steal from you. The Internet is a vast complex of interconnected computer systems and any message you send may pass through many systems on the way to your recipient.

System operators, including those providing your Internet service and your recipients, have the means to monitor your communication along the way. The federal Electronic Communications Privacy Act makes it illegal for them to do so without your permission unless you are using your employer's system or you are suspected of damaging the system or harming another user. Be careful not to sign away your right to privacy as a condition for obtaining an Internet account.

Because the Internet makes online communication so available to others, you should only send credit information to companies that use some form of *encryption* to make sure that your message is scrambled and unintelligible to anyone but them. They should prominently display on their Web site the fact that they have such encryption in place to ensure a *secure online transaction*.

Do not include credit or other sensitive information (such as your phone number, address, social security number, driver's license, or passwords) in any unencrypted online communication, such as chat room discussions, e-mail, Internet newsgroup postings, your online biography, or your *Internet service provider* (ISP) member profile.

You should also be aware that all public postings you make to Internet newsgroups are archived for anyone to search using the *search engines* DejaNews (**www.dejanews.com**) or AltaVista (**www.altavista. digital.com**). In addition e-mail advertisers use *newsgroup* postings as sources of names and e-mail addresses for solicitation. If you go into so-called semiprivate chat rooms available on commercial online services (such as America Online) and some Web sites, other chatters may be recording all that is typed in by participants for future distribution. Even your private e-mail messages can be copied or redistributed by your recipients.

Many commercial Web sites make you pay to access their information. You have to decide if it is worth what they are charging you. You may be able to find similar material elsewhere for free. Web sites can afford to provide so much free information to Internet users because (1) they earn money from advertisers whose banner ads are sprinkled throughout each site, and (2) some "charge" you by requiring that you fill out information they can use for marketing purposes. These sites might issue you a password upon filling out their survey that allows you entry into areas forbidden to casual browsers. Just remember that you do not have to answer any question you don't want to. The worst that can happen is that you are denied access to a site.

The Internet includes another clever little trick to unearth information about you—*cookies*. These are little strings of characters that Web sites deposit in your Internet browser's cookie file to track your movements through cyberspace. When you go to a particular site that you've been to before, the site scans the cookie file on your computer's hard drive to find the characters it deposited. This allows the site to adapt its banner ads to what it knows about your interests based your previous visits. Some cookies are for your convenience, encoding your password to a particular site so you don't have to reenter it each time you go there. For the most part, cookies are used for target marketing purposes by vendors who customize their sites based on your personal information.

To find out about what kinds of information you inadvertently release to others when you surf the Net, visit the Center for Democracy and Technology site (**www.cdt.org**). The following sites teach about cookies and provide software that can automatically delete cookies in your file: PrivNet, Inc. (**www.privnet.com**), Privacy Software Corporation (**www.wizvax.net/kevinmca/**), and JunkBusters (**www.junk-busters.com**). You should also know that Internet browser programs can be set to alert you when a domain tries to insert a cookie into your file. For example, in Netscape Navigator 3.0, under "Options" select "Network Preferences," then "Protocols." Click the box next to "Show an Alert Before Accepting a Cookie." Check your browser program's manual or Help file to find out how to manage your cookie file.

The Privacy Rights Clearinghouse (**www.privacyrights.org**) neatly summarizes your privacy rights in cyberspace.

As we tour through the following automotive sites, I will point out which are in the business of providing information or unbiased reviews of vehicles and which are in the business of selling vehicles or financial services to you.

Some sites are not in business at all. They may be government-run or hosted by consumer advocate groups, car clubs, or individuals. Anyone who wants a forum to share his or her views can set up an Internet Web site, so you must be skeptical of opinions expressed by anyone who is not officially representing an organization that you trust. This is especially true of people posting to newsgroups and chat rooms. They sometimes can provide valuable answers to your questions, but they might also have a hidden agenda, an undisclosed affiliation with a business, or be drawing on their limited experience and understanding of the industry.

One way to distinguish among the kinds of sites out there is to look at the domain name. This is the portion of an Internet address you see between the "**http://**" and the next forward slash (/). For example, **www.bigbucks.com** is a commercial site because it ends in ".*com*." Government sites, like **www.ftc.gov** have ".*gov*" to identify them. Nonprofit organizations have site addresses like **www.helpful.org**, ending in ".*org*." Individuals and groups using their college or university server have domain names ending in "*.edu*" for educational. Other individuals or companies have Web sites on their Internet service provider's server, whose domain can end in "*.com*" or "*.net*" for "network."

You can discover what company or individual owns a particular site by visiting InterNIC (**www.rs.internic.net**), the government-licensed company that regulates the registration of domain names. This might be a good place to visit to find out who you are dealing with.

The more you know about the source of your information, the better you will be able to judge its validity and usefulness. In one click you may go from touring a free informational site to one of its advertisers asking you to buy something. Internet advertising claims also tend toward hype: All promise that they are the lowest priced with the highest quality. The best thing to do is comparison shop without committing any money to any company until you feel comfortable doing so. Otherwise gather what you've printed out from researching on the Internet and take it into the business of your choice to use when negotiating.

SIGHTSEEING TOUR

To help guide you through the automotive world of the Internet, I have created a Web site, CyberWheels (**www.cyberwheels.com**). It provides links to a wide array of automotive sites by category. Using CyberWheels as a starting point, we'll look at a few different types of sites. If you use Netscape or Microsoft Internet Explorer, you should add CyberWheels to your browser's bookmarks or to your list of "Favorite Places" if you use America Online. This will make it easier to go back every time you pick up this book. In case you choose not to use CyberWheels as a guide, the *URL (uniform resource locator)* or *Web address* for each site we discuss will be listed in parentheses following the site name so that you can navigate on your own.

PRICE GUIDE SITE

Find the button on the CyberWheels site for Edmund's (**www.edmunds.com**) and click on it. You will see a screen that looks something like figure 4.2.

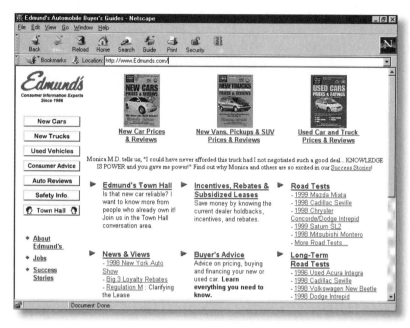

Figure 4.2 Edmund's

Because Internet sites are constantly updated, the Edmund's home page on your screen may look different but it will retain its main functions. Significant changes that take place on all recommended Web sites will be noted at CyberWheels (**www.cyberwheels.com**) on a regular basis. I chose Edmund's because, as a company founded in 1966, it predates the birth of the World Wide Web by decades. During that time it has built a solid reputation for providing objective, reliable new and used car and truck prices in its regularly printed guides. These are still available for purchase, as you can see along the top of the screen.

Down the left side of the screen are buttons that you can click on to take you to different parts of the Edmund's site. The *New Cars, New Trucks,* and *Used Vehicles* buttons take you to the site's searchable databases of vehicle prices. The information in these databases corresponds to Edmund's printed guides. However, the Web information is more frequently updated and easily accessed. Choosing the buttons for *Consumer Advice, Auto Reviews,* and *Safety Info* lets you read or *download* articles devoted to the various subjects under these headings. The *Town Hall* button allows you to enter the site's chat room to converse in real time with others by typing remarks or questions. You may always choose to remain silent and watch the conversation flow by.

This site is also designed to keep the links to advertisers' sites from dominating its own home page. You must scroll down the page to get to the buttons leading to what Edmund's calls its partners. Their advertisements are sprinkled much more liberally throughout the vehicle price reports, however. You may also read about the company's history and the principles that guide it. The lower right quadrant of the screen gives the latest road tests of new vehicles and information about available rebates and incentives.

GOVERNMENT SITE

Now let's go back to CyberWheels and find the button for the *National Highway Traffic Safety Administration* site (**www.nhtsa.dot.gov**). Click on it and you'll see some version of figure 4.3.

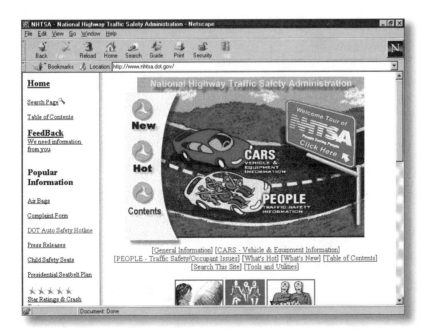

Figure 4.3 National Highway Traffic Safety Administration

This site provides a wealth of information about vehicle safety features and other facts to keep you and your loved ones out of harm's way when driving. If you have any problems with your vehicle, you can lodge a complaint by clicking on the *Complaint Form* link on the left side of the screen. The large graphic on the right half of the screen is an image map, which allows you to click on items within it to go to connected Web pages giving information on either vehicle features or safety precautions people can take. This site is especially useful if you want to study the safety record of a particular car you are interested in. It also can tell you what models have been recalled.

MANUFACTURER SITE

After heading back to CyberWheels let's check out a flashy site of a car manufacturer. Click on the link to the Cadillac site (**www.cadillac.com**) and when its home page comes up, look for the button for its *Interactive Design Studio* (see figure 4.4).

Figure 4.4 Cadillac [©1998 General Motors Corp. Used with permission]

This screen shows Cadillac's four 1998 models and allows you to enter the Interactive Design Studio to customize a Catera by choosing exterior and interior colors, wheel rims, and many other possible options. You can see what your car would look like and then get a manufacturer's suggested retail price for the package. Manufacturers' sites are great for obtaining specs and glossy photos of their vehicles, locating dealerships, and learning about the company. You may check out the rates available from their associated financing companies for loans or leases, but you may be able to beat those figures, as we'll show you in chapter 9.

FINANCING CALCULATION SITE

Go back to CyberWheels and click on the *CarWizard* button to take you to this site designed by *LeaseSource* to help you decide whether to lease or buy. Its direct address is (**www.carwizard.com**). It should look somewhat like figure 4.5.

Figure 4.5 CarWizard

We will be going through this site in depth in chapter 7 when I cover the ins and outs of leasing. The left column of buttons will take you to the heart of the site, in which you can calculate just what your favorite vehicle will cost you in monthly payments whether you choose leasing or buying.

BUYER SERVICE SITE

Our final stop on this little tour is Autobytel.com (**www.autobytel. com**). It should look similar to figure 4.6.

This service also offers lots of information on a wide range of vehicles for you to consider before you decide whether to place a request with its FasTrak service to have participating dealerships send you a bid on the vehicle you choose. We will revisit it later in the book as well.

I hope by now you have a sense of the riches in store for you on the Internet. There are many other kinds of sites available, as you can see by browsing through our site guide in chapter 14. Just remember to surf safely.

Figure 4.6 Autobytel.com [©1998 Autobytel.com Inc. Used with permission.]

The smart way to use the Internet is to gather information from several sources for each aspect of the automotive transaction that interests you. *Never* provide any sensitive information to any recipient company that you don't trust or that does not use encryption to handle its transactions. Remember that sites providing straightforward pricing information and product reviews have links to advertisers who will try to sell you their services. Use our site, CyberWheels (www.cyberwheels.com), as your gateway to the best automotive sites.

Chapter Five

Buying a New Car the Internet Way

"Ere you consult your fancy,
   consult your purse."
—Benjamin Franklin

Too often people worry about things they cannot change while letting others take over what they should be able to handle themselves. When it comes to the imposing task of buying a new car, many people grit their teeth and hurtle through as quickly as possible, burdening themselves with needlessly steep car loans for all of the extras the dealership talked them into. Sadly, their mistakes may cost them many additional hours at work to make their payments, time they could have spent with their families driving around in the dazzler they purchased. Or worse, their credit suffers when they can't pay on time. When they try to sell back the car, they realize that they owe more on it than it is worth. Rather than having equity in their vehicle, it becomes a liability.

Isn't your financial solvency important enough to learn how to buy at a reasonable price? Can't you find better uses for your hard-earned money than overpaying for your car? To become a savvy consumer, you must first figure out exactly how much you can spend. That means dealing with three separate aspects of the new car buying transaction: the value of your trade-in, the cost of the new car, and the terms of financing.

I have broken these up into separate chapters to reinforce the notion that they are distinct transactions. You can find out what your current car is worth in chapter 8 and comparison shop for financing in chapter 9. You may find that conducting both of these transactions on the Internet before even going to a dealership is your best move. That's because you will obtain the true market value for your current car and when you add it to the amount of the loan you secure, you will know exactly how much cash you have available for a new car. Also, the Internet helps you calculate your monthly payments and how long you must pay them so you can adjust your overall budget to accommodate them before a salesperson tries to pressure you. This way you take both of those negotiations out of the hands of the dealership and they can only accept your offer for the new car's purchase price and its options and extras as they apply.

For the purposes of this chapter, let's assume that you have figured out what your available cash is. This is the figure that you will use when we go on the Internet to compare prices. You might find out that your available cash is not enough to afford the kind of car you want. Instead you might realize that repairs and maintenance on your current car are a better investment of your money (see chapter 11). Or you might consider buying a used car instead of a new one (see chapter 6). The best reason to check out the alternatives is that nothing depreciates so quickly as a brand new car. Just driving it off the lot almost guarantees a drop in wholesale value of 40 percent. *Depreciation* occurs more slowly after this initial plunge, so late model used cars in great shape already discounted 40 percent or more will retain most of their value with proper upkeep and moderate mileage.

YOUR ULTIMATE GOAL

 The aim of everything in this book is for you to obtain the most value for your money. The bottom line on new car purchases is that dealerships will accept an offer of $100 over their *Manufacturer's Invoice Price* (MIP) on most vehicles and more are beginning to sell at *invoice*. Whether you purchase a $13,000 Toyota Corolla or a $32,000 Nissan Pathfinder, it matters not! Dealerships can do this because they get a *holdback* (kickback) equal to 2 to 5 percent of the MSRP (manufacturer's suggested retail price) from the manufacturer. In addition, other *dealer incentives* fatten dealer profits that do not appear on invoices.

When a particular model is not selling as well as the manufacturer expected, the manufacturer often provides an incentive in the form of another kickback to dealers to get them to drop their price on the car and sell more of them. But many dealerships prefer to pocket the extra profit when they switch customers to these cars. Dealer incentives can be $2,000 or more on cars that they are trying to promote or on cars that were not sold from the previous year. They are seldom if ever advertised and unless you're an Internet customer, you might never know that they even exist. Stop by the CyberWheels Web site (**www.cyberwheels.com**) and click on the *rebates* link. Find out from the price-guide Web sites that are listed if the car you want has an incentive or rebate being offered by the manufacturer. If so, you can reduce your offer to compensate for the extra profit.

You can also check the same price guide sites for *factory rebates* rather than wade through the hype-filled newspaper ads looking for them. These are payments that the manufacturer makes directly to you for choosing a particular model. Remar Sutton warns in *Don't Get Taken Every Time* that many dealerships use confusing paperwork to get you to sign over your rebate so they can keep it rather than subtracting it from what you owe on the car. Always keep it out of negotiations and have it sent directly to your home.

WHAT IS THE MANUFACTURER'S INVOICE PRICE?

 I told you in chapter 1 that the manufacturer's invoice is a slip of paper showing what the car actually costs a dealership (not accounting for the above-mentioned freebies the dealer gets back). The manufacturer's invoice may also be called a *factory invoice, dealer invoice,* or *corporate invoice*. It is the bill that the dealership receives from the manufacturer for a specific car with a unique vehicle identification number (VIN). The total price of all charges on that invoice is called the *Manufacturer's Invoice Price (MIP),* which includes the base price of the vehicle, *destination charges,* regional advertising assessments, and other costs such as vehicle options. Note that the MIP is not the *base price* of the vehicle, which is its price without options or other charges attached to it. *Take note:* Some dealerships have been trying to sneak a fee for *dealer prep,* which does not appear on the invoice. It is just another little trick they use to try to grab an extra hundred dollars. *Don't pay it.* Only pay the dealership for the legitimate expenses that appear on the invoice.

Now let's get an overview of what you should do to use the Internet to buy a new car.

NEW CAR PURCHASE STRATEGY

1. Honestly evaluate your available cash by researching the value of your trade-in and locate the best financing terms using the Internet.

2. Study the car you want and competitors in its class using Internet price guides, reviews, and safety assessments. Print out copies of the manufacturer's invoice versus manufacturer's suggested retail price for the car and its options.

3. Contact a few Internet auto buying services to determine if they have already negotiated deals for $100 to $300 over invoice for the car you want.

4. Chat with other auto buyers on the Internet who live in your area and ask them to recommend dealerships that serve Internet-informed buyers.

5. When you are ready to deal, choose larger dealerships over smaller ones because they are more likely to have established Internet programs to work with you.

6. Telephone the sales manager first and identify yourself as an Internet customer. Let him know what vehicle you want and how much you are willing to pay for it. Also verify the financing terms you expect based on your credit strength.

7. Avoid using your car as a trade-in; you will usually make at least 20 percent more if you sell it privately.

8. Avoid extended warranties and maintenance contracts.

9. Ask the dealership to confirm your conversation and the terms of your deal with a fax or e-mail.

10. Take a test drive in the vehicle before you sign any contracts.

11. Before signing your contract, obtain the authentic invoice for your vehicle's VIN from the dealership and compare the figures to those on your Internet invoice.

Let's go over each of these steps in greater detail.

Step 1: Calculate Your Available Cash

As discussed above, to keep your roving eyes from lighting upon a car that will cause you financial ruin you should figure out your available cash in advance. Chapter 8 will show you how to determine the best price for your own vehicle and chapter 9 will take you through financing. Just remember that auto loans are serious long-term commitments, so do not sign one lightly. The more cash you can put into a car up front, the less money you'll waste on interest payments. This applies to the length of the loan as well: If you can afford the higher payments of shorter-term loans, less of your money goes toward interest. Also remember to budget for an increase in your automotive insurance if your fancy new car is worth significantly more than your current one. This is also the time to figure out if leasing is a better alternative than buying (see chapter 7).

Step 2: Research the Car You Want

Doing your homework was never as enjoyable as it is now that there is the Internet. Check chapter 14's subject heading "Manufacturers" for an assortment of car makers' Web sites, many of which provide razzle-dazzle multimedia presentations of their vehicles along with specs and dealer locators. These sites are basically advertisements, so be ready for plenty of hype. The prices they offer are invariably the highest: manufacturer's suggested retail prices for the automobile and its options. However, they may alert you to manufacturer rebates or other promotions they are offering to consumers.

To see what I'm talking about, let's do a little surfing.

A Manufacturer's Site with Virtual Technology   Only seeing is believing. The Internet has been making great strides in developing virtual technology, which gives you the ability to explore an environment in three dimensions. In just a moment you will be virtually "walking around" the Toyota Camry LE, whose invoice price you will check on the next site we visit. You can open the Camry's door, sit in the driver's seat, and look around at the control panel, the ceiling of the car, and the back seat. You will almost believe you are in a real car.

Manufacturers and dealerships are currently offering 3-D *photo bubble* and *Quicktime VR (virtual reality)* walk-arounds so you can experience nearly everything the showroom model offers except the new car smell. Let's begin at CyberWheels and take a look at one fantastic site by clicking on the *Toyota* hot button in the manufacturer section (or go directly to **www.toyota.com**).

The Toyota home page will invite you in. Once inside, click on the *Vehicles* icon and you will be given more information about your car of interest than you ever thought possible. There are great photos, interviews, articles, live chats, and the very impressive virtual showroom. Click on the *Virtual Showroom* icon and after it downloads, off you go into another dimension (see figure 5.1)! You may need to download updated *plug-ins* to be able to benefit from all the new technology, but don't worry, it's as easy to do as clicking on your mouse!

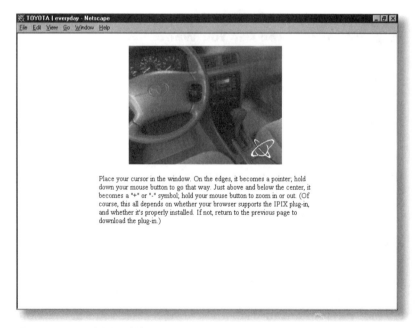

Figure 5.1 Toyota's Virtual Showroom

While you are visiting the Toyota Web site or any other manufacturer's Web page, you will have the opportunity to link to their franchised dealerships' home pages. There you may find the available stock they have in new and used vehicles and other useful information like their operating hours and locations. Some local dealerships have developed their own 3-D virtual showrooms that are impressively informative and enjoyable to use. But beware of dealership Web sites that request your name, phone number, and possibly your social security number so they can get you into the showroom as a conventional sales customer. Don't take the bait.

Factors You Should Consider When Researching Vehicles   Once you have figured out your available cash, you want to make sure you spend it on a vehicle that is a good investment. You'd like your new car or truck to provide you with years of dependable driving with minimal need for repairs. A car that requires expensive replacement parts or gets low gas mileage can greatly add to your ownership costs over time. You should also consider how much insurance will cost for your chosen vehicle. Other important factors include how well the vehicle stacks up against the competition regarding safety, workmanship, and road handling. You may also be interested in such considerations as a vehicle's styling and desirability. It pays to learn how well past models of the same vehicle have retained their original value.

By doing a thorough background check, you may save yourself a lot of aggravation in the long run, as Scott Presser, an associate professor at Cal State University, found out. Scott wasn't looking to impress his colleagues or neighbors with a fancy new automobile. All he wanted was cheap, reliable transportation. He chose the Kia Sephia after borrowing his friend's Sephia GS. He liked how the vehicle handled and was pleased with its gas mileage. And this car was definitely within his budget. But before committing to the Kia, Scott checked out its crash test results on the Insurance News Network site (**www. insure.com**). According to the site, the Kia Sephia 1997 model received an overall "poor" rating in crash tests performed by the Institute for Highway Safety. Because Scott did his homework, he was able to research other cars in the same class as the Sephia before making his final decision.

Other sites you can visit for reviews of vehicles that interest you are listed in chapter 14 under the heading "Reviews." There you will find such sites as the online versions of *Motor Trend* (**www. motortrend.com**) and *Consumer Reports* (**www.consumerreports.org**) as well as other sites offering road test reports and feedback from actual owners. Find out about a vehicle's safety record from the National Highway Traffic Safety Administration (**www.nhtsa.dot.gov**).

Getting Down to Business   When you've decided on a few specific makes and models that strike your fancy it's time to get to the heart of the matter: money. Chapter 14 provides a list of sites under the heading "Price Guides" so you can find out what your favorite vehicle really costs. Let's go back to the price-guide site we visited in chapter 4, Edmund's (**www.edmunds.com**), to price the 4-cylinder automatic Toyota Camry LE.

Now click on the *New Cars* icon at the top of the page. Edmund's will take us to a list of manufacturers. Click on the *Toyota* icon. The next stop will be the *Toyota Cars* page. Look down the list of all the current available Toyota cars and click on *Camry LE (automatic)*. From there we go to our final destination, the Toyota Camry LE *(automatic)* page. I visited the page for the 1999 model year for the figures mentioned here.

The Web page provides an amazing compilation of facts, details, and evaluations about this car. Check out the *Vehicle Information Menu* at the top of the page. The *What's New* hot button will give you all the changes that the Camry LE has undergone since the previous year's model. Click on the *Pros and Cons* button and you will be able to read honest and direct evaluations of the vehicle. Then further down on that column you have other great hot-button points of interest: *Edmund's review, Competing Models, Warranties, Specifications & Safety Features, Insurance Costs,* and *Financing Information.* If you look at the *Competing Models* list, you'll see the other cars in the Camry's class: Chevrolet Lumina LS, Dodge Intrepid ES, Ford Taurus SE, Honda Accord LX, and Subaru Legacy 2.5GT. This makes it easy to do side-by-side comparisons of comparable vehicles.

As you scroll down the page you will eventually get to the real bottom line: the MIP (manufacturer's invoice price) and the MSRP (manufacturer's suggested retail price) for the base car and all of its accessories. At the time of this writing, the new Toyota Camry LE 4-cylinder automatic was sold to dealers at an invoice price of $17,699 (may vary slightly by region) and the MSRP was $20,218—a difference of $2,519.

Note that Edmund's also tells you the dealer holdback, in this case 2 percent of the basic invoice, or $354.

But Edmund's gives two more costs to the dealer that must be added on. The destination charge is $420 for transporting the car from the factory to the dealership. Manufacturers may sometimes overcharge dealerships up front on paper for this service and refund part of it back to the dealer in the future. The dealer, however, just passes the entire cost on to you. The second cost is the dealer's share of Toyota's national advertising. According to Edmund's this is 1 percent to 3 percent of the MSRP depending on geographic region, $202 to $607 in this case. So the MIP for this Camry would be between $18,321 ($17,699 + $420 + $202) and $18,726 ($17,699 + $420 + $607), with a profit from the holdback of $354. Meanwhile if you paid the MSRP, you would hand over $20,638 ($20,218 + $420).

There are a few more costs the dealership bears in addition to the MIP we calculated: costs of local and regional advertising, selling, preparing, displaying, and financing the vehicle. Preparation includes the cost of putting gasoline and oil in the car in order to drive it from the factory onto the truck that transports it. This usually costs under $50. Dealerships pay financing costs when they don't own the cars on their lot but *floor plan* them. By floor planning a dealership gets a loan from a financial institution to afford to stock many more cars than it could with its own cash reserves. When a car is sold, the dealership has to pay off its loan on that car.

For its list of options, Edmund's conveniently includes the same option codes used by the manufacturer. As you pick and choose your way through these, notice the markup from invoice price to MSRP price. My visit to Edmund's showed Toyota charging $499 for a wood dash that cost $335, nearly a 50 percent markup. A "premium 3-in-1 combo" radio was selling for $500 when it cost them $375, a 33 percent markup. This used to be pure profit for the dealerships, but not any more.

By printing out the page, you have the information at your finger-tips to put together your dream car at invoice prices. If you heed the advice in the Edmund's review, you might move up from a V-4 to a V-6 engine. And its *What's New* statement alerts you to the new option of side-impact airbags. And you can take heart that Edmund's called the 1998 Camry "the new standard for midsize sedans."

You may want to take note of the auto buying, finance, insurance, and warranty companies that advertise their services on the Edmund's page. Sometimes they blend in so smoothly it's difficult to notice where straight information from Edmund's ends and the advertising begins. For example, the *Insurance* section of the car report I viewed merely stated the obvious: Rates vary according to many factors. Then it suggested you call its advertiser, Geico Direct, for an insurance quote. You should always be alert to the Internet's cozy blend of editorial and advertising content.

But you should not rely on a single price guide's report. Their numbers should only differ because they might update on different time schedules but the formats of their presentations differ and some include more information than others. I visited the Kelley Blue Book site (**www.kbb.com**) to see if the numbers were any different for the 4-cylinder automatic Camry LE. It provided the exact same base vehicle invoice price of $17,699 and destination charge of $420, as well as the MSRP of $20,218. All of the option invoice and suggested retail prices were identical as well. However, Kelley does not include information about holdbacks and factory-to-dealer incentives that Edmund's provides. In fact, both of them omit mention of another kickback to dealers that Toyota offers, a Toyota Dealership Association (TDA) fee of usually 1 percent of MSRP. It is a cost passed on to consumers and reimbursed to dealerships. How do you figure them apples, Toyota?

I'd like to take a moment here to address Internet auto information services. I encourage all of the information services to address the holdback/kickback issue more thoroughly. Some services discuss holdbacks and some do not. Kelley Blue Book avoids discussing the dealer association fees and holdbacks so consumers do not get "confused." I ask Kelley Blue Book and others to forget about our possible confusion and share the whole truth about the extent of dealer profit. Edmund's does discuss incentives, rebates, and dealer holdbacks, giving consumers more of the news they can use. But they still could improve their coverage by including items like Toyota's TDA fees in their invoice reports.

Step 3: Contact Internet Auto Buying Buying Services

You can get the best deal on a new vehicle by collecting all the information you need and then conducting negotiations with a dealership yourself. But if you still want to save thousands of dollars on your car purchase with absolutely no inconvenience, you can use an Internet *auto buying service*. Auto buying services contract with franchise dealerships to provide set prices on new and used cars to customers. These kinds of companies predate the World Wide Web, but since its inception they have made use of the Internet to provide good value to the informed consumer who doesn't mind paying indirectly for their services. They charge the participating dealerships fees on a monthly or per car basis and dealer price quotes will be on average $200 to $800 over what you could receive by doing it yourself.

The auto buying service Web sites are free. You are not obligated to buy from any dealer that gives a price quote, although the services prefer that you are a serious buyer and not merely collecting information. But how can you become a serious buyer if you do not collect information? Auto-buying service Web sites are listed in chapter 14 in the "Buying New Cars" section. As you saw in chapter 4, a favorite is Autobytel.com (**www.autobytel.com**), which provides plenty of information in addition to offering its FasTrak auto-buying system. Other popular sites you may have heard of are Microsoft CarPoint (**carpoint.msn.com**) and AutoBuyer (**www.autobuyer.com**).

It will take you less than fifteen minutes to query five auto buying services. You choose the vehicle make and model, provide your contact information, and wait for a price quote. If you have your own e-mail address, the auto buying services will e-mail you back and pass on your request to one of their franchised dealerships nearest you. A dealership's Internet representative will usually call within twenty-four hours and will quickly give you every bit of information that you ask for.

Sample questions you may want to ask the dealer Internet representative:

- Do you have the car I am looking for in stock?
- If I am ready to purchase the vehicle today, will you sell it at manufacturer's invoice? (or $100 over invoice?)
- I got the dealer incentive amount for this car from the Web; will you deduct this amount from the invoice?
- I would like you to pre-approve me on the phone for the manufacturer's subvented (subsidized) interest rate; can you take the application now? If the manufacturer approves me, how soon will the car be available for contracting?
- Can you deliver the car with the contract to my home or office?

It's just the way it should have been done for years. The buying service will also e-mail you to make sure the dealership is giving you good service. For once you can really feel like royalty when you buy your new car. It boils down to the old saying "Throw the ball up and wait to see who catches it first." Dealer representatives available through Internet auto buying services generally treat you with respect, knowing that they are vying for your business on the basis of price and value rather than sales flimflammery.

You will probably find that some small cars like Toyota Tercels, Honda Civics, and Ford Escorts are usually sold through auto buying services for approximately $200 over the MIP while larger cars are a bit higher. You may decide it's easier to accept this relatively small markup than to have to negotiate with a dealership for a price at invoice or even lower. The best price quote you receive will result in payments that are attractively low for the class of car you choose if you make sure you do the rest of your homework by finding the best financing terms and the true market value of your trade-in.

Another benefit of such services is that you can learn which of your local dealerships is set up to handle Internet customers. In my studies of the Los Angeles area, nearly every dealership I contacted at random had Internet departments.

Step 4: Chat with Other Auto Buyers on the Internet

Before the advent of the Internet, where could you go to chat with a group of other people who were also car buying? Just try comparing notes with fellow car buyers on a dealership lot and see how long it takes for the salespeople to jump in. Now you can check chapter 14's "Chat Rooms" heading for Web sites that provide these online gathering places.

I recommend this step because not only is it great fun, but you can get valuable information from other new car buyers. Those who reside in your area can point you to dealerships with Internet departments that served them well or steer you away from less reputable places. In addition to the auto reviews and consumer-tested recommendations from Internet services, sometimes you need to hear honest personal testimonials from actual owners of the vehicle you'd like to drive. Just remember that everyone is entitled to his or her opinion and the Internet is where many go when no one at home will listen to them anymore.

Step 5: Choose Large Dealerships

Choose larger dealerships over smaller ones because larger dealerships will probably have established Internet programs in place to handle your no-haggle purchase. They'll happily whisk you into an office to keep you from mingling with those customers who are ready to pay thousands of dollars more than you. Unlike small mom 'n' pop dealerships, their high-volume operations can afford to make low-grossing deals if they have enough of them. Small places often need to wring out every last penny from each deal they make.

Step 6: Call the Sales Manager

Even when you have decided to approach a particular dealership, you need not physically enter the place to begin making a deal. You can save time and effort by telephoning the dealership and identifying yourself up front as an Internet customer. If this is a dealership with an Internet department, they should turn you over to their Internet consultant. Otherwise speak to the sales manager and say you are ready to deal. Identify the specific model car you have chosen and how you want it equipped. Never start your conversation with a conventional salesperson.

Here's the big moment. You've already calculated what the invoice cost is for your vehicle complete with the options you've just specified. Go for it and name that price as what you're willing to pay. If the dealer representative will not go that low, decide whether you are willing to bargain up to $100 or higher than that invoice price. I would not recommend going above $100. Instead, approach another dealership with your offer.

How likely are dealerships to accept your rock-bottom bid when they have padded their deals for so long? Many are quite ready to do so. In April of 1997, I compiled information for a case study to determine the "ease of negotiating an Internet deal on the phone" in the Los Angeles area. I found that after calling fifty different dealerships, I was able to obtain my Internet "$100 over invoice" price for most vehicles, along with reasonable financing terms, in a matter of minutes and most dealerships were willing to deliver the vehicle at no additional cost to my home or office. I did not discuss trade-in information so as to standardize the process.

I did my homework for financing and lease rates before I made my calls and you should too (see chapters 9 and 7 respectively). Make sure you have already used the Internet to calculate how to achieve the level of monthly payments you'd prefer before you call. Once you've comparison shopped for the lowest loan rates on the Internet you can use those figures on the phone to the dealership. Let the dealer representative know what bank rates and loan term you are expecting, and if the dealership's financing offer cannot match that you should seek financing elsewhere.

Step 7: Avoid Trading in Your Car

Dealership salespeople are full of stock stories about the horrors of trying to sell your own car: shady characters coming to sellers' homes, checks bouncing, and buyers suing sellers at the drop of an exhaust pipe. Even if everything goes smoothly, they warn you of the drudgery of spending all your spare time making appointments to show your car to a stream of strangers.

But if you knew you could earn an additional $2,000 to $3,000 by putting a For Sale sign on the window of your car, placing an ad in the local paper, or advertising it on the Internet, would you do it? The general rule is that you can sell your own car for at least 20 percent more than you would get if you trade it in to a dealership. And if you follow a few precautions, you can avoid those horror stories salespeople use to frighten you. To learn more about trade-ins versus selling your car yourself, see chapter 8.

If you are determined to trade in your car as part of your negotiation over the phone with your chosen dealership, you can try. Some dealerships will do a *blind trade* on the phone, conditional upon their confirmation of the accuracy of the information you give them. But most don't like to take the time involved in assessing your trade-in if you are not in their showroom. This modus operandi will change as Internet-based transactions become more prevalent.

Step 8: Avoid Extended Warranties and Maintenance Contracts

These days most manufacturers already provide comprehensive warranties for their vehicles. The price-guide sites detail exactly what is covered as part of the manufacturer's invoice reports they produce. For example, according to the Kelley Blue Book site, the Toyota Camry LE we priced has the following coverage: 3-yr/36,000-mile Limited Basic; 5-yr/ 60,000-mile Limited Powertrain; 1-yr/12,500-mile Service Adjustment (except New York); 2-yr/18,000-mile Service Adjustment (New York); 5-yr/Unlimited-mile Corrosion Perforation. Note that this was a more complete description of warranty information than Edmund's provided.

The *service adjustment warranty* covers all the minor annoyances like squeaks, rattles, and alignment problems. Covered under the *pow-*

ertrain warranty is the engine, transmission, and rear axle—in other words, the heart and guts of your car. You should check what each manufacturer includes under its *basic warranty*. The *corrosion perforation warranty* guarantees against rusting. With this kind of warranty do you think manufacturers would be sending out cars in need of protection packages like rust-proofing and undercoating?

Maintenance contracts and extended warranties give you more coverage for repairs to your vehicle beyond the manufacturer's warranties. According to Remar Sutton in *Don't Get Taken Every Time,* dealerships love these extra warranties because they cover much less than people believe and dealers often sell you coverage from a questionable firm operating out of a state that lacks strong consumer protection laws. Thus these underwriters are not scrutinized to the same extent as national firms like GMAC (**www.gmacfs.com**). If you feel that you absolutely need an extended warranty, buy one from a recognized national firm.

I'm going to pass along some good advice my dad gave concerning extended warranties: Only get coverage if you cannot afford the consequences of not having it. Take the money you would have spent on an extended warranty and put it in a special "disaster account" in the event you would ever need it. When you pass the extended warranty period without using it, you can pocket a good deal of extra cash. If you absolutely need to purchase a warranty, it can be negotiated. Usually the dealership will discount the warranty 25 percent to 30 percent. And stick to a contract from a national brand. (See sites listed under "Warranties" in chapter 14.)

Step 9: Get Written Confirmation of the Price Quote

Ask for written confirmation detailing the terms of the deal you've worked out over the phone. It's always good business practice to get everything you want in writing. If you have your own Internet account, you can ask for your confirmation by e-mail; or, if you have fax capabilities, ask for it to be faxed to you. Despite everything we told you about how dealerships refuse to give conventional customers price quotes in writing, they almost always give Internet customers written confirmations upon request. Otherwise, shop elsewhere.

Step 10: Test Drive

For this step you actually have to get out of your pajamas and go into the dealership. Take a test drive of the car you negotiated to buy. Even new cars sometimes have rattles or sluggish breaks or uneven alignment. You can even test-drive a few cars to make sure yours feels right. Remember that *you are in complete control now*. You can relax because the price has already been decided and the test drive is not a prelude to a horrendous negotiating marathon. If you identify any problems, now is the time to get the service department to fix them—before you hand over the money and drive away. The dealership is much more likely to make your repairs a priority when they still need something from you.

Step 11: Check All the Figures on Your Contract

Obtain from the dealership their manufacturer's invoice and confirm that the vehicle identification number (VIN) on it matches the one on your new vehicle. Also check to make sure that it shows the name of the manufacturer and the name of the original dealer that purchased it (it may have been traded from a different dealer). This document's figures should match those on your Internet invoice.

Don't let your excitement overwhelm your good judgment this close to the finish line. Go over every single form to make sure it is completely and accurately filled out before you sign. On the *buyer's order* you are about to sign, confirm the accuracy of the date, the year of the car, the make and model of the car, the VIN number, the asking price, taxes, and other fees. If you do decide to trade in your car, confirm the same identification for it as well as your trade allowance and the difference between the *trade-in allowance* and the new car's asking price. If you are financing, check the accuracy of the total amount to be financed, the number and amount of monthly payments, and the *annual percentage rate (APR)* of your loan.

You will also have to sign a mileage statement attesting to the exact mileage now on your new car, and your trade if you have one, so the dealer doesn't try to tamper with the odometer and fill in a lower number when reselling the car. Guess what? You'll be the one who is liable. You may also have to sign over limited powers of attorney so the dealership can legally transfer title to the car. If you decide to accept dealer financing, it means more paperwork to sign. Scrutinize your finance contract for the same finance information listed on your buyer's order.

A Success Story

I recently received an elated phone call from my old friend Jim Cassidy, with whom I had discussed the contents of the book as I was writing it.

He gushed, "It works! It *really* works! I got the car last night for $100 over manufacturer's invoice. You are right, this is amazing!" I was not surprised that the purchasing process I recommended to Jim worked so effectively but I was curious to find out exactly what Jim had done to buy his new car, so he recounted for me each of the steps he took.

"Well, first I did as you told me to, I plugged in my computer," he laughed. (Jim is a bit of a clown.) "I went to the World Wide Web to the CyberWheels site and clicked on the *Edmund's* button. I was fairly certain that I was in the market for a Lexus ES 300. But to be completely sure, I checked out the 'Competing Models' section on the Lexus ES 300 page and found four other models listed in its class: Acura 3.2TL, BMW 328I, Chrysler LHS, Infiniti I30, and Oldsmobile Aurora.

"Within ten minutes I was able to get information on these cars and do a more detailed comparison than I could have imagined. I even viewed the cars on the 360-degree photo bubble viewer and was able to see every detail of the car inside and out. I was about to switch to the I30 but I really love the lines on the ES 300 and, after checking the manufacturer's invoices, I decided that the ES 300 was more affordable. Edmund's also alerted me to the fact that the ES 300 had a whopping $2,000 rebate that I was not aware of.

"Once I knew the car I wanted, the rest was cake. I visited the brokers listed on the CyberWheels Web page and asked for bids, which took all of four minutes. I found out the locations of my local dealerships from the Lexus Web page in another minute and a half, checked out a few lenders' interest rates and even found an insurance company offering rates lower than what I am paying now!

"Ha!" Jim shouted exuberantly. "This system is wonderful! The tough part was containing my excitement about driving my new car home. I called my local Lexus dealership and let the manager know that I was going to purchase an ES 300 today and that I already had an approved bank loan. I gave him all of the options I needed and offered him $100 over invoice for it. He promised to have the contract waiting for me when I arrived at the dealership. The car was prepped and waiting when I arrived. I took a test drive, kicked the tires, and drove away in a matter of minutes. Now that's the way to buy a car. No pressure, games, or hours of agony. It was unbelievable!"

Congratulations, New Car Owner!

If you have followed the steps in this chapter (along with the tips in chapters 7, 8, and 9), you will be the owner of a brand new vehicle that should give you pleasure for years to come. While you take pride in the car's aesthetic value, sleek design, excellent handling, and innovative safety features, you should also pat yourself on the back for getting a great deal! You deserve congratulations for bypassing one of the most ingenious, labyrinthine schemes for separating you from your money ever devised.

NEGOTIATING UNDER MANUFACTURER'S INVOICE PRICE (MIP): FOR BORN NEGOTIATORS ONLY

Now that you are in the proverbial driver's seat, you may want to turn the tables and play hardball with the dealership by holding out for a price *below* invoice. If you are the aggressive type who enjoys negotiating or if you want revenge for the many years you've suffered under dealership tyranny, here is your chance at sweet payback! Offer a price below invoice and stand firm. You may have to leave and return to the dealership two or more times in order to bargain down to the point where the dealership actually gives up some of its holdback or other kickback fees to meet your price.

I have successfully completed "under invoice" deals with some dealerships, but currently a deal for a car at invoice is as far as most will go. In time, as the Internet pushes the industry toward greater price competition, those operating with greatest economies of scale may start negotiating under invoice.

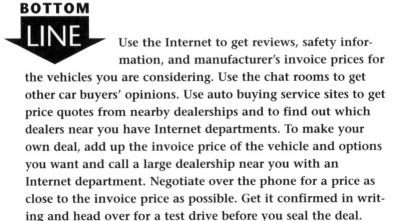

BOTTOM LINE Use the Internet to get reviews, safety information, and manufacturer's invoice prices for the vehicles you are considering. Use the chat rooms to get other car buyers' opinions. Use auto buying service sites to get price quotes from nearby dealerships and to find out which dealers near you have Internet departments. To make your own deal, add up the invoice price of the vehicle and options you want and call a large dealership near you with an Internet department. Negotiate over the phone for a price as close to the invoice price as possible. Get it confirmed in writing and head over for a test drive before you seal the deal.

Chapter Six

Internet Strategies for Buying Used Cars

"Patience is bitter but
the fruit is sweet."
—Jean Jacques Rousseau

U sed car dealers hold a special place in the public's mind as devious charlatans scheming to shackle unsuspecting customers with worthless scrap heaps for exorbitant prices. I ask you, on your last used car purchase, how do you know whether you got a good deal? Unless you obtained insider wholesale information, *you don't know!* You may be proud of how much you bargained the dealer down but you still have no idea what the dealership made from your sale. Many car dealers have long held the credo: "The more profit extracted from the customer, the greater the customer's satisfaction."

They could get away with this because until the advent of the Internet, used car prices were well insulated from scrutiny. However, the online presence of honorable business people is transforming the industry. For this reason the Internet strikes fear into the heart of every unscrupulous used car dealer. There are now numerous Web sites offering the public the same insider information on used cars that was once jealously guarded by auto professionals.

This chapter will help you use the Internet to figure out the most important piece of inside information: the *wholesale* and *retail price* of the used vehicle you are considering. However, I emphatically caution: *Buying a used car with the Internet requires more work than buying a new one.* There are a few more steps involved because even used cars from the same model year may be in markedly different condition. Variations in maintenance, mileage, and optional equipment can affect their price.

For a new car, you need look up only one invoice price. For a used car, you need to research that vehicle's true *market value* using the same tools at the disposal of the dealerships: information services and auto buying services that are now available to the public for *free* on the Internet.

Used cars are typically more profitable to a dealership than new cars because the true wholesale prices of used cars vary for each individual car, giving dealers a lot of leeway to build in profit. Often car owners accept much less than the fair trade-in value for their cars, which adds to dealer profits. According to J. D. Power & Associates, the average new car costs consumers approximately $19,000, while the average used car costs about $10,000, yet the average profit dealers make on used cars is double what they make on new cars. This means that you have the potential to save much more on a used car by cutting into that bloated profit margin.

The price range of a used car is based on a complex combination of the vehicle's attributes and options, including its mileage, the size of its engine, the type of transmission it has, its accessories, and its structural integrity. Online information services that take these attributes and options into account include Kelley Blue Book (**www.kbb.com**), Edmund's (**www.edmunds.com**), and AutoSite (**autosite.com**).

These guides provide a price range bracketed at the low end by a wholesale price and at the high end by a retail price. Kelley Blue Book calls these *low blue book* and *high blue book,* respectively. Edmund's describes them as *trade-in value* and *market price* and AutoSite refers to them simply as wholesale and retail prices.

Despite the availability of these price guides, it's difficult to determine exactly just how much the dealership pays for its used cars. It is safe to assume that the price it paid is hundreds or thousands of dollars lower than the fair low blue book recommended by Kelley Blue Book, the trade-in value cited by Edmund's, or the wholesale price listed by AutoSite, because most car owners don't realize the true value of their trade-ins and give them up for too little money.

 Dealerships often try to purchase a trade-in from a customer for at least $2,000 under low blue book. That means that if the low blue book of a 1995 Honda Civic is $5,500, the dealership will probably offer $3,500 for it. In the lingo of dealerships, when you bring in your vehicle to be appraised, the dealer representative will *book the trade* and the number that they arrive at will be low Kelley Blue Book value. If they can actually pay you the standard $2,000 under low blue book value, it is considered a fair deal, but if they pay a good deal less than that, they *steal the trade*. And this is all legal!

 But price guides offer only one tool. You should also adhere to the following rules whether you plan to buy a used car from a dealership or from a private party.

The most important rules of this used car-buying game are to be patient and do your Internet homework. Salespeople gain the advantage when customers seek immediate gratification and are ignorant about the bargaining process.

TEN PRINCIPLES OF BUYING A USED CAR ONLINE

1. Distinguish between what you need and what you want.

2. Research the used car's model year for recalls, J. D. Powers' customer satisfaction, and ratings.

3. Determine the fair market value of the used car by checking with the automotive online services.

4. Obtain the car's VIN (vehicle identification number) and research it online for information about prior ownership.

5. Be patient! Recognize and overcome any urge to buy impulsively. Never rush into any deal.

6. Have the basic functions of the car checked by a mechanic.

7. Offer a lowball price. Some sellers have cash flow problems and will sell their vehicle for below what they paid for it.

8. Thoroughly test-drive the car on the highway and city streets.

9. Notice how clean the interior is, which indicates how well the car was cared for.

10. Look for telltale signs that the car was in an accident or has had major structural damage, such as evidence of repainting and welded seams on the inside of the car body.

CASE STUDY: A NATURAL-BORN NEGOTIATOR

Debbie Brooks, a Los Angeles trial attorney, visited a Toyota dealership to buy a used 4-Runner. The sticker price was $22,540. The low blue book value of the car was $18,497 and the dealership actually paid $15,000 including refurbishing costs. Because the dealership paid over $3,000 less for the 4-Runner than the low blue book value, they *stole the trade* with a hefty profit. Debbie offered $15,000 for it. She also requested $2,000 on her twelve-year-old trade-in with 135,000 miles on the odometer. Her trade-in booked at $800. She wanted to use her trade-in as a down payment for the 4-Runner *and* pay thirty-six monthly installments of $361!

Ridiculous, you say? That's what the salesman said, too, but it didn't stop our Miss Brooks. The salesman reminded her that the dealership was not in business to lose money and then counter-offered $21,500 for the car and $200 for the trade-in. Debbie rejected the offer. She finally got up and started to leave the dealership.

The dealership's manager reopened the negotiation process and offered Debbie $21,000 for the car and $600 for the trade-in. "My friend, my friend," exclaimed Debbie, "Are we here to deal, or to waste each other's time? What is your bottom price?" The closer responded, "If I give you a number that you are happy with, will you drive away with the car tonight?" "Of course," retorted the attorney. The closer returned with his "absolute best price": $16,500 and $1,000 for the trade-in.

Note: In order for the dealership to offer the customer $1,000 for a trade-in valued at $800, the difference would have to be absorbed into the profit margin on the 4-Runner. Since the dealership paid $15,000 for the 4-Runner, offered $16,500, and was willing to absorb $200 for the trade-in, this deal would have made the dealership $1,300.

This profit margin is still fairly low by current industry standards, but Debbie rejected the offer because she knew that she would get the lowest price only after the dealership stopped trying to negotiate with her. Debbie then lowballed them with an offer of $15,800 and $1,200 for the trade. Of course, the dealer representative wasn't about to lose money on the deal, so Debbie shook the salesman's hand and left the dealership. She knew that she reached the bottom line because *she was permitted to walk.*

The next day Debbie Brooks got a call from the original salesman asking, "What will it take to make this deal?" She responded, "$16,000 and $1,000 for the trade." "Impossible!" shouted the salesman. "Well then, take the offer to your boss," said Debbie. On the third day, the dealership accepted Debbie Brook's offer and she purchased her beautiful used 4-Runner for $300 over cost.

Debbie Brooks finally got a great deal by using her superior negotiating skills to beat the dealership at its own game. But did it have to take three days and countless painful hours to accomplish? That's a miserable way to shop. If Debbie had researched the 4-Runner on the Internet before walking into the dealership, she could have wrapped up the deal in just a matter of minutes, including the finance rates, warranties, and after-market accessories.

You will *not* need to learn the art of negotiation as practiced by Miss Debbie Brooks to purchase used cars on the Internet, but a rudimentary understanding of how to negotiate a deal is helpful. Let's do some Internet surfing and work through a real-life example of purchasing a used car. When doing your own surfing, you may find that the Web sites look a bit different than they do in the following illustrations because the Internet is continually being updated.

EXERCISE

For this exercise you will use Autobytel.com to obtain a listing for an actual 1997 Ford Explorer for sale at a car dealership in your area. The listing should include information about all of the car's attributes and options as well as the seller's asking price. Then you will calculate its true market price with the help of the Edmund's, Kelley Blue Book, and AutoSite Web sites. Also, you can compare these price estimates against what other local dealers and private sellers are charging for similar cars. Finally, I will show you how to make the offer on this vehicle.

Step 1: Obtaining an Asking Price for a Real Vehicle

Fire up your web browser and head out on the superhighway to CyberWheels (**www.cyberwheels.com**). Click on the Autobytel.com button. Its URL is **www.autobytel.com** if you go to it directly (see figure 6.1).

Figure 6.1 Autobytel.com [©1998 Autobytel.com Inc. Used with permission.]

Scroll through the list of manufacturers until you see Ford. Type your zip code in the appropriate box and click on the *Click to Begin* button. The next screen will prompt you for the model of the Ford vehicle you are looking for and whether you want a new or used one.

Click on the *Used* button. An exhaustive list of Ford Explorers will be displayed showing the year of each vehicle along with its price and mileage. Just choose one by clicking on it. Autobytel.com will give you a full description of it and which dealer is offering it, including the vehicle information number (VIN), which you can use to run a check on the history of that particular car's ownership as described below.

Print this description page for yourself, as we will refer to it often as we begin to analyze this vehicle on three different Internet car-buying services Web sites. The object of this exercise will be to see if the car you picked is really a good buy. First, let's head out to . . . Edmund's!

Step 2: Price Guide Comparisons
Edmund's Go back to CyberWheels and click on the Edmund's Web site button or go to it directly at **www.edmunds.com** (see figure 6.2).

Figure 6.2 Edmund's

This Internet auto resource thoroughly describes just about every car available on the market. Click on the *Used Car* button and then type in the make (Ford) and model (Explorer) of the car you are looking for. Color will not affect the price. Don't be too picky, this is just an example. The 1997 Ford Explorer page will show a list of all the models that Ford sells in this class from a two-door Sport to a four-door Limited edition. Click on the *Four Door XLT*. Notice that a new screen comes up. It shows the base trade-in price and the market price. To make the proper price adjustments click on the *mileage adjustment* icon, and after you have computed the price of this Explorer based on its mileage, click on the *equipment adjustment* icon to compute the true market value of the Explorer based on its options.

Edmund's has now given you two prices for that 1997 Ford Explorer: the *trade-in price* and the *market price*. The trade-in price minus about $2,000 is what you can expect the dealership to have paid for the 1997 Ford Explorer in your Autobytel.com description. The market price is what private parties often sell their vehicles for in the classified section of local newspapers. You will need both prices as a point of negotiation.

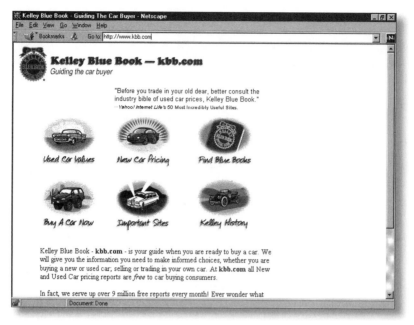

Figure 6.3 Kelley Blue Book [©1998 Kelley Blue Book. All rights reserved.]

Kelley Blue Book Go back to CyberWheels and click on the Kelley Blue Book link or go to it directly at **www.kbb.com** (see figure 6.3).

The Kelley Blue Book home page will prompt you in a similar manner to give the make and model of the car you are looking for and whether it is new or used. The Kelley Blue Book numbers will be similar to the ones given by Edmund's but the jargon will be different. Most dealerships prefer to use Kelley Blue Book because its printed version has traditionally been an industry standard for determining the value of used cars. I frequent the Edmund's guide because it is easier to use, it has the *Town Hall* chat room, and it offers comparable used car prices.

Take the same 1997 Ford Explorer information you got from Autobytel.com. Notice that Kelley gives a low blue book and high blue book value. High blue book is equivalent to Edmund's market value and low blue Book to Edmund's trade-in value.

Let's compare the local dealership's asking price for the '97 Ford Explorer to one more auto information service to see how it compares to the actual fair market price of that vehicle.

Figure 6.4 AutoSite

AutoSite Go back to CyberWheels and click on the AutoSite Web site button or go to it directly at **www.autosite.com** (see figure 6.4).

This Web site is my favorite because I believe that is the most user-friendly of all online automotive services. It is chock full of pertinent auto buying topics and the financial calculation section is more detailed than the other two information services we visited. The AutoSite *Report* includes a schedule of installment payments on its financial section. This will be discussed in detail in chapter 7, "To Lease or Not to Lease?" At last count AutoSite had approximately 100,000 cars and trucks listed in its classifieds section.

Click on the *Search AutoSite Classifieds* button. That will take you to the AutoSite *free classifieds* page. Click on the *Sport Utility* button. Fill out the form with the requested data. This page will ask for the state you are in, the make and model of vehicle, and a few general questions. Enter the 1997 Ford Explorer, as you did at the other sites. Click on the *Search* button and you will be offered a list of cars for sale in your area. Highlight and click on any one of the 1997 Ford Explorer XLT models.

Print it out so we can go back to the AutoSite home page to determine if the dealership's asking price is a fair one.

Take a shortcut back to the AutoSite home page by clicking on the *Previous* button at the top of the screen. Now click on the *Book Value Report* button. You will be prompted to pick a manufacturer, model, and year. Click on the *Click Here* button and you will be prompted to check off the options that are applicable to the vehicle and its approximate mileage. Click on the *Click Here* button and presto! You are given the wholesale and retail values. Now that you have all the information possible about that 1997 Ford Explorer, go back to the AutoSite home page and click on the *Recall* button to see if the manufacturer recalled the vehicle for any reason. Then take a few minutes to browse through the AutoSite recommendation section, which you can find by clicking on *Pro-Picks in the Used Car Market* button.

Now it's time to make a very important decision. How much should you offer for the car? Well, hold on to your lug nuts, we are about to find out after we finish step 3.

Step 3: Compare

Go to other auto buying service Internet sites, local dealer sites, and private party classified-ad sites. Autobytel.com, Edmund's, Kelley Blue Book, and AutoSite are just a few of the many Internet resources that can help you find your perfect dream used car at the best price available. Look in chapter 14, "The Best Auto Sites on the Net," for other Internet sites that represent dealers and private sellers in your locality. You may be able to find local dealership home pages through links from the manufacturer's Web site.

Purchasing from a Private Party   If you are new to the Internet, you may not be aware of the mountain of commerce taking place on it every day. Private parties around the world buy and sell cars from their own personal Web pages or they place ads on the Web pages of auto buying services. Listings often include pictures of the vehicle along with a description of it that is much more detailed than anything you could find in a three-line classified ad in a local newspaper. References to these Web pages can be found on the bulletin boards of Internet service providers such as AOL. You might also learn about such sites by entering one of hundreds of chat rooms that cater to car buyers and sellers, for example, Town Hall, located at **www.edmunds.com** or Auto Talk at **autoweb.com**. I know you will find it fun as well as informative.

Figure 6.5 Carfax

Step 4: Vehicle Identification Numbers

Each vehicle has its own unique *vehicle identification number (VIN)*, which is assigned to it alone. By law, dealerships must supply a car's VIN to any prospective buyer who requests it. It is now possible to use the VIN on the Internet to obtain the car's vehicle history report, which alerts you to certain aspects of the vehicle's condition that would not otherwise be apparent. I highly recommend pulling a VIN report on any vehicle you are about to buy from a private party or dealership for your complete peace of mind. You can go to Carfax at **www.carfax.com** (see figure 6.5) on the Internet to obtain a vehicle history report for about twelve dollars. In chapter 14 you can find a list of other companies that will supply you with this information as well.

What will a vehicle history report tell you? Most of the available reports are divided into three sections: Vehicle Specifications, Vehicle History Details, and Problem Summary. By checking the odometer readings in a vehicle's history report you can determine if the odometer appears to have been "rolled back" to show less mileage than it should.

Vehicle History Details gives information about how the car was used by each owner. Each titleholder has to declare to the motor vehicle department whether the car will be used, for example, as a private vehicle, a lease vehicle, a rental vehicle, or a government vehicle. It also provides emissions inspection records, which illustrate driving patterns.

Problem Summary can include "Potential Problem Found Reports," in which potential problems are identified that may affect a vehicle's safety, value, or performance. If the vehicle was *salvaged,* it was refurbished after being totaled in a serious accident. It might be flood-damaged or tagged with other conditions that may render it worth much less than the seller would like to admit. Although the vehicle history report might bring you terrible news, at least you learn it before you buy.

Now wasn't that easier than the traditional trial by fire that dealerships force you through? No more wasting precious time and gas to run around town looking for the best deal! Or listening to misleading salesmen. Or being detained by dealership *closers.* All you have to do is click your little mouse on the next auto seller's home page. It's that simple!

Step 5: Go to the Dealership or Private Party Selling the Car You Like Best

Contact whoever has the best price on the car model with the characteristics you like. At this point you should ask to visually inspect the car for any obvious damage and take it for a test drive. You may also want to take the car to a mechanic to check out the car's main systems. These actions are not as crucial when buying from a used car dealership as they are when you buy from a private party because most state laws hold professional dealerships legally liable for the cars they sell. In contrast, private parties sell their vehicles "as is," so you have the responsibility to make sure the car is in good shape.

MAKING THE OFFER

Savvy buyers in the automotive market know they never have to pay retail. Cars are bought and sold by comparing *wholesale* pricing. Dealers will offer customers at least $2,000 under wholesale price for trade-ins, and, as we discussed earlier, they'll often try to pay even less. That means they will sell to you for less as well.

Larger dealerships may be easier to work with than smaller ones because they are willing to cut profit margins and make up for it in volume of sales. In contrast, small dealerships must rely on high markups on each car. Deal directly with the sales manager and immediately identify yourself as an Internet customer. He may already have an Internet clerk working with him. Offer to pay the dealership 5 percent under the wholesale price (low blue book) for the car you want. This will give them a fair profit margin and your deal will likely to be accepted. If you purchase from a private party you should offer 15 percent or more under the wholesale price because they don't have the overhead that dealerships have. The dealership will usually include a limited warranty (required by law in most states) and may spend some of its resources to recondition the vehicle before it is sold. The private party will usually sell the vehicle "as is" rather than spend any money in reconditioning costs because the sale is final.

This chapter arms you with all of the information you need to beat the dealership at its own game. Salespeople may call you a *mooch* behind your back and challenge your methods, but some will respect you for your uncommon abilities and insights. But even if you are not respected, your thirty-minute investment of time on the Internet will save you thousands of dollars if you stick by the prices you've identified as fair market values for the car you wish to buy and the one you are trading in. Remember, you are not car shopping to find a mate or make lifelong friends; your purpose at the dealership is to buy the car you desire at a fair price and prevent the dealership from digging deep into your pocketbook.

BOTTOM LINE Use the Internet to research the type of car you are interested in by going first to Autobytel.com, then to Edmund's, Kelley Blue Book, and AutoSite. These sites allow you to calculate the car's fair market value. Check out online auto buying services and classified ads to see if any come close to this price. When you find a seller, pull a VIN report using Carfax and have a mechanic check the car. Offer 5 percent under the fair wholesale price to a dealer selling the car or 15 percent to a private party.

Chapter Seven

To Lease or Not to Lease: A Hard Look at the Numbers

"A man is his own easiest dupe,
for what he wishes to be true he
generally believes to be true."
—Demosthenes

You've seen the ads for leasing cars: $99 a month will put you behind the wheel of a new Honda Civic, $189 gets you a new Accord. It sounds enticing, yet too good to be true. Is it? Well, the first thing to realize is that leasing means renting. You only have use of the car for the length of the lease. It is not yours to keep. Therefore the money you spend on a lease might be better spent to purchase the car outright. Almost everyone has heard leasing horror stories from business associates, friends, or family members in which they were subjected to extra charges, hidden fees, high *early lease termination fees,* and expensive repairs on vehicles they don't even own.

But leasing may serve your needs if you know the facts before you enter into a contract. This chapter shows you what's behind this rapidly growing segment of the industry, compares how leasing stacks up to buying, defines the key terms in leases, and takes you step-by-step through an Internet site that helps you calculate the lease you want. First, I offer a cautionary tale about a consumer whose ignorance cost him big time.

CASE STUDY: GARTH'S GREAT DEAL

Garth Messer despised car salespeople ever since he met his first one at age twenty-one. That dealer charged him a 22 percent interest rate and

$400 over the car's MSRP (manufacturer's suggested retail price) because, the dealer claimed, as a first-time buyer he was a high risk. In truth, first-time buyers are entitled to the same interest rates, rebates, and other discounts as established buyers as long as they can prove they have adequate income. Three cars later and still feeling that dealerships were getting the best of him, Garth was out for sweet revenge.

This time he decided he would lease rather than buy. His neighbor just purchased an Avalon and was thrilled that he bargained the dealer down to $1,800 under the MSRP. Garth figured he would beat the dealership at its own game by getting the same price, only for a lease. He was pumped and ready for battle. He walked up to the sales manager and demanded to get the same deal or he would leave immediately. The dealership complied. Garth signed the contract and drove off the lot victorious. He was so ecstatic about his success, he told everyone he knew. Far and wide, people heard of Garth's great deal. But how great was it?

Garth did pay $1,800 under MSRP, but the invoice price of the Avalon was actually $3,200 under MSRP. The dealership made close to $1,400 on the purchase price alone. But Garth's biggest loss was on the terms of the lease itself, where the dealership made $1,875. He did not realize that with his good credit he could have negotiated a much lower interest rate.

 Sadly, Garth got taken for a ride once again because he only paid attention to one part of the deal: the purchase price. The salespeople must have high-fived each other after he drove off the lot. The benefits of Garth's good credit ended up in the dealer's pocket through a practice called *building the reserve*. Building the reserve is a common tactic in which the dealership works to get the consumer to accept a higher interest rate than what the bank considers a fair market rate. The difference between fair market and the higher rate is called the *reserve*. The bank kicks back to the dealership a portion of the profits derived from the reserve.

THE LEASING INDUSTRY

Leasing makes billions of dollars for the auto industry in the United States. The profits are staggering. It's not surprising that so many promotions try to convince you to lease rather than buy your vehicle. Advertisements and salespeople make very convincing arguments for leasing: You can drive a more expensive car than you could afford to buy; you can have a new set of wheels every two or three years instead of having to wait much longer.

 But these benefits must be weighed against the hidden mathematical tricks dealers use to keep the consumer in the dark. Leasing offers an ideal playground for the retail auto industry to engage in covert shenanigans; it is the final frontier of consumer deception. Even those who work for an automotive retailer dare not ask in-depth questions about the *lease* because its complexity often baffles the finance department, much less rookie sellers. Dealerships merely instruct their salespeople to say, "It's just a smart way to get a car," trusting the naïve customer to accept it. For many years this strategy worked.

Now sites on the Internet are lifting this veil of confusion. By revealing the meaning behind the leasing terms, these sites show you why salespeople so often pressure you to lease cars rather than buy them. As my microeconomics professor wisely taught me, "The best way to figure out people's motives is to follow the money." The Internet lets you follow the money to the conclusion that leasing vehicles is usually much more profitable for a dealership than selling them.

But it doesn't have to be that way. You can now negotiate for the terms you want and avoid expensive added fees and hidden costs. Depending on your circumstances, leasing can be a viable option—if you are well-informed.

LEASING VERSUS BUYING

If you're not sure whether to lease or to buy, consider the following:

1. How long do you plan to keep your car? If you like to drive a new vehicle every three or four years, leasing would make more sense than an outright purchase. If you trade in a car too soon after buying it, you will not have accumulated enough equity to permit a reasonable trade-in. Also, you may not wish to keep the car longer than the warranty period, in order to

avoid the expense of repairs and maintenance. If you plan to hold on to your car for five years or longer, purchasing makes more sense than leasing.

2. Would you like to drive a better car than you can afford to purchase outright? Leasing a vehicle may be appropriate for you if you'd prefer smaller payments on a more expensive vehicle than a loan would allow. Leasing payments are smaller because you're only paying for the part of the car you use—its depreciation during the loan period—rather than the whole car.

3. Has trouble in your credit history made banks reluctant to extend you auto loans? Some banks may offer a customer with poor credit a short-term twenty-four-month lease rather than a long-term loan. But you should be careful of the limitations the lender places on you.

4. Are you prepared to make monthly car payments into the fore-seeable future? Because leasing does not build equity in your vehicle, this is not the path toward owning it debt free. Exercising your option to buy at the end of a lease is usually much more expensive than a loan to buy the vehicle outright. Also, if you experience a financial hardship that forces you to cancel the lease early, you could face some extremely stiff penalties.

5. If you are making your decision on behalf of a business, do the tax deductions of leasing benefit you more than owning? Because of the rate at which cars depreciate, their value as company assets may be less than the deductions obtained from leasing.

The Consumer Task Force for Automotive Issues, founded by Ralph Nader, offers a free publication to consumers to help calculate leasing costs. The "Reality Checklist" is a no-nonsense, seventeen-question worksheet that can help you decide if leasing is right for you. It is available for free on the Internet at **gopher://gopher.essential.org:70/00/ftp/pub/csrl/reality_checklist**.

WHAT IS A LEASE?

From *The American Heritage Dictionary of the English Language:*
lease (lēs) noun

1. a. A contract granting use or occupation of property during a specified period in exchange for a specified payment. b. The term or duration of such a contract.

2. Property used or occupied under the terms of such a contract.

An auto lease is a rental agreement. It guarantees you the right to use a vehicle for a specified amount of time in return for a certain amount of money that may be divided up into periodic installments. You pay for the amount the vehicle depreciates in value while you are using it, plus an additional amount of profit for the leaseholder.

PARTIES TO THE LEASE

There are three parties to the lease—the seller, the *lessor* (the bank or leasing company), and the *lessee* (you, the driver). Let's look at the role of each and then define the terms that make up the lease.

The Seller—This is usually the automobile dealership, or in some instances, the vehicle's manufacturer. In a lease transaction, the seller does not actually sell the car to you, although you take delivery of the vehicle. The actual sale and transfer of the title on the vehicle is made to the lessor. The seller acts as an agent representing the lessor.

The Lessor—This is the vehicle's real owner. The lessor purchases the vehicle from the seller (dealer or manufacturer), receives title to the vehicle, and then turns the vehicle over to you for a specified period of use at a fixed monthly rental rate. Depending on the type of lease, when the term ends the lessor may sell the vehicle to you or take possession of it to sell to someone else. Lessors take many forms, including vehicle manufacturers with their own leasing companies, private investors, and of course, banks.

The Lessee—You are the lessee. You take delivery of the vehicle from the seller but you do not own it. Instead, you make monthly rental payments to the lessor for use of the vehicle. When the lease period ends, you either purchase the vehicle from the lessor or return it to the lessor with no further obligation.

TWO TYPES OF LEASES

When you lease, you will have a choice between an *open-end* (sometimes called a finance or equity lease) and *closed-end* lease (also called a net or fixed-cost lease).

Open-end Lease

If you choose an open-end lease contract, you are betting that the car will retain much of its value and that its resale price will be higher than what the lessor projects it to be. The lessor's projection is defined as the *residual value*. At the end of the lease, when you turn the vehicle back in, it is appraised to determine its current market value. The lessor then compares the appraised value to the residual value that was determined when the vehicle was contracted. If the vehicle's appraised value is equal to or greater than the residual value, you can walk away from the deal and owe nothing. But if the appraised value is less than the residual value, you must make up the difference in cash. Of course you have the opportunity to purchase the vehicle at its appraised fair retail value. This is known as an *option to buy*.

Take note that it is highly unlikely the lessor will underestimate the residual value of any vehicle compared to its eventual appraised value. In other words, it's much more likely that you will wind up paying what is known as a *balloon payment*. Due to this fact, open-end leases are responsible for much of leasing's bad-boy reputation.

Closed-end Lease

A closed-end lease is much safer for the consumer because you are not responsible for making up any difference between the initially estimated residual value and the actual appraised value. Instead you have the option of returning the car when the agreement expires or purchasing it for the residual value. Because you do not assume any of the risk in anticipating the car's market value, your monthly payments on a closed-end lease are usually higher than those on an open-end lease.

DIFFERENCES BETWEEN LEASING AND A CONVENTIONAL LOAN

There are major two differences between leasing a vehicle and purchasing it through a conventional bank loan:

- With a lease, the lessor is actually the party that purchases the vehicle to rent it to you. In a conventional loan, the bank loans you the money to purchase the vehicle and holds the title as collateral.
- With a lease, you pay the purchase price of the vehicle minus what the lessor expects to sell the vehicle for, plus a profit for the lessor. On the conventional loan you agree to pay the entire purchase price of the vehicle minus the down payment plus interest.

FIVE IMPORTANT LEASING TERMS

There are five leasing terms that you need to understand before we calculate the lease. Some of them are subject to negotiation:

1. Capitalization cost
2. Lease term
3. Fees and taxes
4. Residual value
5. Money factor

Capitalization Cost

The *capitalization cost* (*cap cost* for short) is the purchase price of the vehicle used to calculate the lease. Some unscrupulous salesmen may tell you that a lease is always based on the MSRP of the vehicle. This is not true. You need to negotiate the price of the car using Internet tools just as you would if you were actually purchasing it (as covered in chapter 5). You should aim for a cap cost that is $100 over dealer invoice.

Lowering the cap cost of the car by $2,000 or $3,000 from MSRP will significantly lower the monthly cost of the lease.

You can also lower the cap cost with a *capitalization cost reduction* (*cap reduction* for short) by making a down payment or trading in your old car. This will lower your monthly payments. Leasing "teaser" ads like the one offering a Honda Civic for $99 a month usually require huge cap reductions, sometimes totaling thousands of dollars. However, making a high down payment defeats the purpose of leasing because unless you purchase the car at the end of the lease term, you are losing the money you put into it. The best lease deals combine a low monthly payment with no money down.

Taxes and fees are also added to the total purchase price in the lease. Sometimes the bank will try to get these fees up front from the customer as part of a fee called the *drive-off* instead of including them in the lease. Some banks require a minimum drive-off, which includes the first month's payment and tax and license. They insist that the drive-off does not constitute a down payment. Don't believe it. Savvy lease consumers with good credit never pay any form of down payment.

Customers with weak credit may be asked to pay a deposit, which may amount to one or two months' payments. The best strategy for leasing is to include all fees in the contract with a true zero down and no drive-off.

Lease Term

The *lease term* is the length of the contract, which typically ranges from two to five years. The longer the lease term, the lower the monthly payments and the higher the total interest paid. The shorter the lease term, the quicker you can move on to a new car, but since you are renting rather than buying, you have no asset in the vehicle. You will be paying a premium price for very little return. Instead the dealership gets back a nearly new, low-mileage vehicle to resell at a huge profit. Salespeople may deny it, but you have no equity in your car at the end of the lease unless you exercise your option to buy.

So what lease term makes sense? Two years is just too short for what you must pay, although the industry is determined to convince you otherwise. A four-year lease or longer may take you beyond the vehicle's warranty. Once the vehicle is out of warranty, you risk expensive repair charges. You don't want to pay for repairs on a vehicle that does not even belong to you. I recommend limiting the lease term to cover the full original warranty of the car (and please, no extended warranties or maintenance contracts). Typically, most auto companies will warranty their vehicles for thirty-six months and up to 36,000 miles, whichever comes first. Therefore a thirty-six-month lease is my suggestion.

Fees and Taxes

Fees and taxes also factor into the total cost of the lease. States and some localities impose various sales taxes. They are usually levied only on the lease's down payment and the monthly payment. Vehicle *title and registration fees* also vary within each state. The *disposition fee* is often buried in the lease contract and few dealers call attention to it. This fee, which can amount to several hundred dollars, is paid at the end of the lease period if you do not exercise your option to buy the car. Look closely in the contract for the disposition fee and tell the dealer to eliminate it.

The *assignment fee* (also called the *acquisition fee, lease initiation fee,* or *lease inception fee*) is charged by the leasing company to pay for the commissions earned by the dealership. Typically $350, it is unnecessary and, in most cases, will be waived if the customer recognizes it. Insist that the fee be waived or absorbed into the dealer *margin*. If the salesperson refuses, just pleasantly offer to leave. The dealership should be satisfied with the profit that it makes solely from the sale of the vehicle.

Residual Value

The vehicle's *residual value* is the figure that represents the estimated value of the car at the end of the lease. Subtracting the residual value from the initial cap cost (purchase price) gives you the amount of depreciation expected during the term of your lease. The residual value is important for calculating the monthly payment. The lower the residual, the higher your payment. The vehicle residual value is expressed as a percentage of the retail price (MSRP) of the car. Typical residuals range from 35 to 70 percent and will vary depending on the length of the lease. To determine residual value, most lessors use standard automotive industry references, such as Kelley Blue Book (**www.kbb.com**), that are readily available on the Internet.

Money Factor

The *money factor* is a decimal number that is used to calculate the lease payment. To convert this number to an approximate interest rate, multiply by 24. Example: A money factor of 0.0037 converts to an interest rate of approximately 8.9 percent. The money factor varies by the model of vehicle chosen and the length of the lease. This effective annual percentage rate (APR) is the most important factor in comparing costs. The only purpose I can see for dealers to use the money factor instead of an interest rate is to keep the consumer from fully understanding leases. Dishonest salesmen will tell their customers, "APR does not apply to a lease." It's sad how many people have been duped by this line and have overpaid for interest as a result.

LEASE VERSUS LOAN TERM EQUIVALENTS

Lease	*Loan*
Capitalized (Cap) Cost	Sales Price
Cap Cost Reduction	Down Payment
Net Cap Cost	Amount Financed
Sales Tax	Monthly Sales Tax on Payment
Residual	
Monthly Depreciation	Principal Amount of Payment
Money Factor (lease charge)	Interest Amount of Payment
Base Monthly Payment	Payment Before Tax
Lessor	Bank
Lessee	Borrower

USED CAR LEASING (RENTING)

Interest in the new car leasing market has spilled over to the used car market. Each year more people are leasing used cars. By the turn of the century some predict that over one million used car leases will be written. Is this good for the consumer? Let's explore this issue further so you can decide whether used car leasing is right for you.

COMPARING THE NEW AND USED CAR LEASE

New and used car leases vary from each other in two ways: the money factor and the depreciation rate. You might assume you would get a better deal leasing a used car than a new car because the used car will not depreciate as quickly. But that is only half the story. The new car will depreciate an average 40 percent over two years while the used car will depreciate about 18 percent. However, the money factor (interest rate) will generally climb much higher on the used car. Manufacturers don't subsidize the rate on used cars like they do on new cars.

CALCULATING THE LEASE RENTAL RATE

In chapter 14 you can find a list of Web sites that offer calculators that will replicate the following calculations for you. You can use the following five simple calculations to get a rough idea of how much your lease will cost you so you can understand what these calculators are doing.

1. Capitalization cost
2. Monthly interest charge
3. Monthly depreciation and taxes
4. Monthly total
5. Total payment

For this example I will use the following hypothetical figures.
Capitalization cost (total purchase price): $25,000
Residual value: $13,000
Lease term: 36 months
Money factor .0035 (equivalent to 8.4 percent APR)

1. **Cap Cost (total price of the vehicle)**   The negotiated price of the vehicle plus taxes and fees minus capital reduction (down payment and trade-in). In this example the cap cost is $25,000.
2. **Monthly interest charge**   The total of the purchase price plus the residual value multiplied by the money factor.
   ($25,000 + 13,000) (.0035) = $133
3. **Monthly depreciation and taxes**   The purchase price minus the residual = the depreciation.
   Depreciation divided by the term = depreciation per month.
   $25,000 − $13,000 = $12,000
   $12,000 ÷ 36 = $333
4. **Monthly total**   Depreciation per month plus the interest per month = monthly payment.
   $333 + $133 = $466

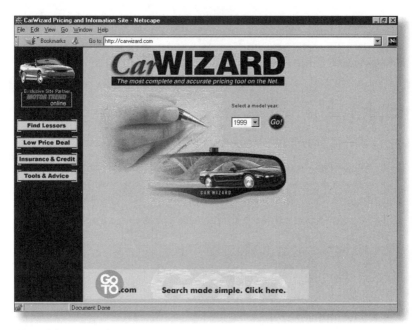

Figure 7.1 CarWizard

5. **Total Payment**   Total monthly payment multiplied by the term of the lease (monthly payment multiplied by the term of the lease (months) = total payment
$466 × 36 months = $16,776

   To calculate the lease terms on your chosen vehicle, you will have to find its capitalized cost, residual value, and money factor from the Internet. So let's jump online and see what's available to help you nail down the figures for your ideal lease.

USING THE INTERNET TO CALCULATE LEASE RATES

It's time to surf the Net and find out what leasing bargains are available. You will be amazed to realize how simple it is to shop for leases on the Internet. In just a few minutes you will learn how to save hundreds or thousands of dollars on just the financing end of the lease. So fasten your cyber-seatbelts.

For this exercise we'll use the same make and model vehicle from previous Internet excursions, the Ford Explorer XLT 4-by-2.

Step 1: Go to CarWizard

Let's start at CyberWheels (**www.cyberwheels.com**) and click on the *CarWizard* button (or go to it directly at **www.carwizard.com**).

In my estimation, CarWizard (see figure 7.1) is one of the five best auto Web sites. And in just a moment you will see why.

Notice on the far left the listings of everything you might ask about leasing. There is a *hot button* (when you press it you move to another screen) for locating lessors, finding a low price deal, securing insurance and credit, and other tools and advice. In the center of the page is a box where you have to specify the year of the car you are looking for. Click *Go!* and it will take you to a page that displays hot buttons to do payment calculations, vehicle comparisons, vehicle value retention, and much more. If you have not yet decided on the make and model you want, you can use these options to help pinpoint the best vehicle for you.

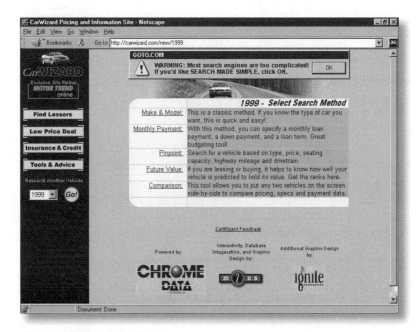

Figure 7.2 CarWizard Search Screen

The *Monthly Payment* button will help you select vehicles that stay within your budget. By clicking on the *Future Value* button you will be advised about the best and worst vehicles to lease based on the residual value that is assigned to each vehicle by different banks. The *Comparison* button will help you compare all makes and models of vehicles in the same class. Not only are you able to compare vehicle features but also financing and lease rates and pricing.

Step 2: Select Make and Model

Click on the *Make & Model* button. Here you will find an exhaustive list of manufacturers that produce cars, trucks, and vans. Click on the *Ford Utility Vehicles* button. That will take you to the next Web page, where you will see two hot buttons displayed—one for the Expedition and the other for the Explorer. Click on the *Explorer* button. A list of all the Explorer models that Ford Motor Company produces will be displayed. There is a 4-door AWD (four-door All Wheel Drive), 2-door 4WD (two-door four-wheel drive), a limited model, and many others (see figure 7.2).

Click on the 4-door XLT 4WD and shazam! You'll see a picture of the vehicle and all of its options. It's important to take note of these options because in the next screen, CarWizard will let you check off the options that are important to you and automatically calculate their total cost. You are also presented with two important costs of the vehicle: the wholesale and retail base prices. We are now ready to go to the *Options* button on the left-hand side of the page.

Step 3: Select Your Desired Options

Click on the *Options* button at the top of the page and you'll be taken to a page that features a picture of the Ford Explorer, with its base price listed underneath. As you select your required options, the site will automatically calculate the total cost of all that you have chosen. Make sure you also check the boxes that apply to your state's registration fees and emissions standards. Notice that when you are done, all the options you have selected have been totaled at the bottom of the page, under *New Totals*.

Print out this page for your records. You will certainly be interested in exploring the *Tech Specs, Warranty & Rebates,* and *Road Test & Safety* options that are available along the top of the screen. For now though, click on the *Residuals & Factors* button.

Step 4: Review the Lease Data

The *Residuals & Factors* page lists the pertinent financial data for this lease. Notice how the residuals and money factors change based on the number of years financed.

These are only average rates for you to use as ballpark figures. Later we will visit some leasing company and bank sites to find specific rates in your area. But the CarWizard rates are fairly close to the national rates. This Web site gives the *Automotive Lease Guide*'s (ALG) rates for residual values. The *Automotive Lease Guide* provides the wholesale industry standard for leasing.

When you go to the leasing company and bank sites, you can compare the competitive residual values that they give you to the ALG values from the CarWizard site. The higher the competitive residual a site gives you, the better the lease deal it is offering. That is because they are estimating less depreciation on the car you drive, so they expect it to retain more of its resale value. The other factor you have to consider is the interest rate the leasing companies or banks offer you along with the residual value. *You want to combine the lowest interest rate with the highest residual value.*

Print out this page for your future reference. You need some of the residual values from CarWizard when you visit the AutoSite Web site in step 8 of this exercise.

This page also gives you a payment table for your lease payments. The more money you put down up front, the lower the payments will be. You can also see how the payments break down for lease terms of 24, 36, 48, or 60 months. Please note that CarWizard uses the vehicle's manufacturer's suggested retail price to calculate all of these figures. Your actual payments should be substantially lower based on how far below the MSRP you can negotiate your cap cost to be.

Step 5: Compare Lease Payments

Let's move on and compare lease costs for vehicles in a certain class. Go back to the *CarWizard* home page, select the model year, and click *Go!* From the next screen, select *Monthly Payment*. In the form that appears, enter the down payment you are willing to make, the lease term, and the payment range that falls within your budget. Select the vehicle type and click on *Begin Search*. CarWizard will offer you a list of vehicles that fit your requirements. Now you can compare the specific monthly lease and purchase costs of these vehicles. The beauty of CarWizard is its simplicity.

Step 6: Value Retention

Value retention is very important in choosing which vehicle to lease. If the banks and leasing companies feel a specific vehicle will retain a high value over the length of the lease, they will give the car a low depreciation value. The smaller the depreciation value, the higher the residual value and the lower your monthly payment. If you are going to lease, lease a vehicle that will give you nice low payments!

What are the two best utility vehicles to lease in 1999? Let's click on the *Future Value* button on the Select Search Method screen. Choose "Utilities" under the vehicle type, "36 months" under least term, and "15 Best" under limit results. Using this criteria, the top two vehicles we found were the Mercedes Benz M class 4-door all-wheel drive and the Ford Expedition.

Note: Some Web site calculators and Web site services will use national average interest rates and MSRPs to figure your monthly lease rates. These default figures could increase your monthly rate considerably depending on the size of the loan. To protect yourself use Internet calculators that will allow you to fill in your own rates and figures.

Step 7: Vehicle Comparison

Let's compare car costs. On the Comparison page, you can compare any aspect of two different cars. Choose two vehicles that interest you and you can view a side-by-side comparison. At the top of this page we are supplied with pictures of the selected vehicles. Farther down the page, the lease payments and loan payments are displayed. General specifications concerning the engine type, gas mileage, measurements, and horsepower are listed at the bottom of the page. This feature offers a very convenient method to choose between two models that interest you.

Step 8: AutoSite Calculation Page

Because CarWizard only gives estimates of costs based on MSRP, you cannot use it to calculate what your actual lease would look like for a particular vehicle. To help with this calculation, go back to the CyberWheels site and click on the *AutoSite* (**www.autosite.com**) button.

On the left-hand side of the page, click on the *Loan/Lease Report.* You will be taken to a calculator page with two columns of boxes labeled *loan* and *lease.* Some of the boxes are marked *Req* (required information) and others *Opt* (optional information). You can fill out just the lease column if you have decided you'd rather lease than buy your chosen vehicle. Fill out both to compare the two options.

First type in the total amount you wish to finance in the Taxable Vehicle Price box under both loan and lease—or just one column if you have already decided which method to use. Then type in your state's sales tax in the next box, followed by your desired down payment, the number of months you wish to lease or finance (term in months), the annual interest rate (see chapter 9 on how to find the best rates online), and the residual value you got from CarWizard. After you have entered these numbers click on the appropriate button (*loan only, lease only,* or *both*), and the Web site will calculate your monthly payments and money factor automatically.

GETTING READY FOR BATTLE: NEGOTIATING YOUR BEST DEAL!

 It's important to acknowledge that both emotions and intellect come into play when you decide to lease. We all like to think of ourselves as level-headed, rational decision makers but the truth is that playing on the customer's emotions is the most important factor in selling and leasing cars. That is why many salespeople will not talk to you about the deal until you have taken a test drive around the block. When you enter the dealership you will be emotionally primed for a great deal. Many customers will make an emotional decision to lease vehicles based solely on lower monthly cost and their fantasies of driving a new car every two or three years. I cannot count the number of consumers I have met who have deeply regretted this decision. They wound up in debt because they did not fully understand all the facts about leasing before signing the contract.

To overcome appeals to your emotions, you have to play hardball, using the information you got from the Internet to stand firm. Remember that the object is to pay $100 over invoice for your new vehicle without offering the dealership any additional profit from the lease. The reason they will accept this offer is that dealerships profit from:

1.   A holdback (kickback) they receive from the manufacturer.

2.   The additional dollars that you pay over the invoice price of the car. Although dealerships would prefer to make $4,000 profit over manufacturer's invoice for your next purchase, they would rather accept less than lose you to their competition.

The key to negotiating a lease deal with the salesperson is simply making the dealership match the lowest lease rates that are available on the market. Have all the information you obtained from CarWizard and other Web sites ready when you sit down. When you are armed with the same information the dealership has, they cannot pull the wool over your eyes. Dealerships will accept zero profits from the financing of leases because they've already made a profit on the negotiated cap cost of the car. For the dealership, leasing profits are just the icing on the cake.

Read the lease carefully. Make sure that there are no extraneous fees added to the lease except for tax and license. Remember, by using the Internet you will keep the dealership accountable for the costs of the lease just as you did with the base cost of the car. You do need to keep in mind some very important questions in leasing your vehicle:

● How many miles do you drive per year and how many miles are allowed on the lease? Usually an average of 15,000 miles per year is allowed. You may have to pay an expensive *excess mileage fee* if you exceed that amount.

● Will the lessor (bank) absorb all the tax and license fees in the lease so that you have no out-of-pocket expenses?

● What is the penalty cost for terminating the lease early? Remember that you will be heavily *upside down* on the lease (you owe more money than what it is worth) until you have made at least 80 to 90 percent of the payments. The fee charged for early termination can be substantial.

● If you have a bad credit history, will you need a security deposit?

- Is there a cost for *GAP insurance* in the event of an accident? This would limit your out-of-pocket expenses to just a small deductible. (GAP insurance supplements your own automotive insurance. If you get into an accident in your leased vehicle or it is stolen, you still have to pay off the entire lease. This often adds up to much more money than what your regular insurance provides. GAP insurance covers the rest, except for a small deductible that you must pay. Leasing companies often include GAP insurance as part of the lease, so check to see how much coverage they offer and how much they charge for it.)
- Are there any fees being added to the lease except for possible tax and license that you may be paying for out of pocket?
- Do you really need the maintenance package that the dealership will try to sell you at the time of contracting? I do not recommend it because it is just a way for the dealership to make a higher profit from you.

CONSUMER PROTECTION

Auto-lease disclosure is governed by the eighteen-year-old Consumer Leasing Act, part of the law known as the Truth-in-Lending Act. The Federal Reserve Board Regulation M, revised in 1997, explains the Consumer Leasing Act.

Regulation M applies to leases that are negotiated by individuals for personal or household purposes that exceed four months in length and are less than $25,000. This law does not apply to leases for business or commercial purposes. Regulation M mandates that before a lease is executed, the following disclosures must be made to the consumer:

- A description of the leased property
- The total amount of money due at lease signing, itemized by the type of charge
- Monthly payment information
- Any other charges or fees
- Total of payments
- Payment calculation
- Early termination
- Maintenance responsibilities
- Wear-and-tear definition

- Purchase option
- Fees payable for registration, license fees, or taxes
- All other charges not included in the monthly payment
- Insurance information
- Warranties
- Liens, if any
- Penalty information
- Open-end liability
- Renegotiations, extensions, and assumptions

As our culture becomes more accustomed to purchasing and leasing cars on the Internet, the process will become as easy as comparison shopping for a can of tuna at the grocery store. The Internet leasing sites provide access to the most competitive rates and help you calculate your ideal lease.

BOTTOM LINE Learn the terms involved in leasing contracts and the methods for calculating your true costs to decide if you should lease rather than buy. Then go to CarWizard and AutoSite to use online calculators to determine a fair deal for the vehicle you want to lease. When you go to the dealer, negotiate first for the lowest price for the car, then for terms matching the best deal you could find on the Internet.

Chapter Eight

Selling Your Car on the Internet

"Here's the rule for bargains:
'Do other men, for they
would do you.' That's the
true business precept."
—Charles Dickens

Do you really want to sell your car to a dealership? In chapter 6 we discussed the incredible profits that dealerships make on trade-ins. If wholesale book value is 20 percent lower than the fair market value for your car, the dealership will consider it fair to buy it for 20 percent under that price. For example, if your car's fair market value is $10,000, the average low blue book may be $8,000. The dealership will offer you $6,400, and if they try to *steal the trade,* they will offer you even less.

Let me ask you this: If you could spend a few hours to place some free ads on the Internet, make a few phone calls, and show the car to prospective buyers, would it be worth $3,600? Not many of us make so much per hour at work that we could justify losing that much money.

My first and foremost suggestion for selling your car is: *Do it yourself!* These days, with the Internet at your fingertips, it just can't be easier or more fun to sell your car on your own despite the dire warnings you'll hear from professional car salespeople. Dealerships have been scaring people for too long about how horrible it is to sell cars privately. They say it's inconvenient and exposes you to shady characters, maybe even lawsuits. I will grant that selling cars to dealerships is easier, but it never makes economic sense. And the shadiest people may be found right on dealer lots.

CASE STUDY: THE GOOD SCAM

I will never forget the Morris family, who needed to buy a large van for their very large family. They could not fit themselves and seven children in their five-passenger 1997 Toyota Camry. The family responded to a *100 percent sale* ad, which is very popular in parts of California and certain other sections of the country. The claim of this outrageous scam is that if you have a vehicle that is three years old or less, the dealer will give you—you got it—100 percent of the original selling price of your automobile.

Jack and Judy Morris were ecstatic. They could not believe that they would be offered full value on their original purchase. Jack never liked the Camry anyway because it was in constant need of repair. He was looking forward to unloading it. Judy was happy just to get a van that would fit her entire family.

The salesman, Stewart, was very helpful and charming as he built a rapport with his clients. Jack and Judy listened intently while he explained how the 100 percent sale worked: "We will indeed pay you 100 percent of the total price that you paid for your car minus any costs involved for us to fix wear and tear or damage to your vehicle. Since we are going to pay you 100 percent of what you paid for your vehicle, you wouldn't expect us to have to pay more for any damage or maintenance costs that we must incur. Is that fair, Mr. and Mrs. Morris?"

"Why, of course, Stewart," exclaimed Jack. "As long as your dealership is willing to pay us exactly what we paid for our car minus repairs, we have a deal!" Jack was delighted that he had finally found an honest dealership.

At that point Jack gave Stewart his keys so that his 1997 Toyota Camry could be examined. It had 26,000 miles on the odometer and was clean, with just a few dings (tiny dents) on the driver and passenger doors. Also the electric seats were not working. Jack had paid $21,400 for the car less than two years earlier.

A few minutes later, Stewart reappeared smiling. "Jack and Judy, the manager was a little upset with me about this trade because of the extra work that it will need to get it ready for resale, but because you responded to our newspaper ad he will give you $21,400 for it as promised."

After the good news sank in, Stewart continued: "As you know, you have some body damage on both sides of the car that, of course, will have to be repaired and repainted. The total cost for this is $2,870. The transmission and engine will need its 25,000-mile tune-up, which is $840."

Stewart was far from finished: "The car will have to be detailed and there are three stains on the back seat that have to be cleaned. The detailing and cleaning come to $399. Oh, and the electric seats need to be completely rewired, which is $600, and, lastly, the car needs new tires and a brake job that total $1,432."

He ended on a sunny note: "There were a few scratches on the bumper, but we will let that go if you promise to send us three more referrals. By the way, folks, how would you like us to register your new vehicle? In both your names?"

Judy spoke up right away. "Of course," she said, turning teasingly to her husband, "I am a liberated woman."

Jack chuckled and shook his head. "So, how soon can you have the van ready for us?"

"In just a few minutes," Stewart said with a wink. "Let me get you a cup of coffee while you are waiting."

Synopsis of the Scam

 Although Jack and Judy thought they were getting 100 percent of their car's price, the repairs the dealership claimed it needed added up to $6,141! Their Toyota Camry was actually in good condition with a low book value of $18,400. When they accepted 100 percent of the purchase price for their car minus the reconditioning and repairs ($6,141 total), that left them with $15,259—$3,141 below the car's wholesale market value.

This was a "good scam" because everyone was happy. The salesman was happy because he made a nice commission on the trade-in alone and the dealership was happy because the total deal ended up grossing over $6,500 when the back-end profit from Jack and Judy's purchase of the new van was added in. And the Morrises were very happy because they got back "100 percent" of the price of their old car!

Jack Morris did not forget his promise to the salesman to send in three referrals. Two of his coworkers and his cousin ended up stopping by the dealership to take advantage of the 100 percent sale. You would be surprised how many people end up falling for the scam. The ancient Greek adage, *caveat emptor*—let the buyer beware—never seems to go out of style. Internet buyers and sellers following the simple steps described in this chapter will *be aware* of what they are doing.

PROS AND CONS OF SELLING YOUR CAR YOURSELF

If you are deciding whether to sell your car yourself instead of trading it in to a dealership, there are a few factors to consider—your convenience, time, safety, and salesmanship. To make it worth your while, you must take charge of the process to ensure that you get a fair price, are paid in full, and are not exposed to legal liabilities of any kind. You must become an enthusiastic salesperson, placing your car in the best possible light, because whether you have a creampuff or a junker, a coveted model or a boxy tank, if it runs, it is worth something to someone.

CONVENIENCE

The plain truth is that dealerships offer convenient one-stop shopping. When they give you a trade-in allowance, you are paying for the ease with which you can unburden yourself of your old car while sliding behind the wheel of that new beauty. Drive on the lot in one car, leave in another. What could be simpler? Not much. But you pay dearly for that convenience.

TIME

On the other hand, selling the car yourself requires you to plan ahead to make the best use of your time. If you own only one car and rely on it to get back and forth to work, you want to minimize the amount of time between the sale of your old car and the purchase of your new one. You should be researching everything necessary to buy the new car at the same time you are preparing to sell your old one. It helps if you can gain the financing to buy the new one before you have to part with the old one. However, if you need the money you make from the sale of your current car to help pay for the new car, you might be forced to go without a car for a while. In this case, work out alternate travel arrangements for the interim period.

The stream of inquiries you will field before you find a serious buyer will also take up your time. People may make appointments and never show up. They may not even give you a courtesy call to say that they are not coming. The phone may ring off the hook at all hours of the day or night. It takes time to work with some people on a large purchase before they are willing to finally make up their mind. You can expect to spend more time lining up a buyer if you are holding out for a high price that is at or above retail market value.

SAFETY

When you place a classified ad for your car, you must give prospective buyers a means of contacting you. Usually this is your home or work telephone number. Placing an ad on the Internet gives you the option of being contacted by e-mail. Think through how you plan to meet the people who are interested in seeing your car. It may be convenient for buyers to come to your home, but is it safe? Do you live alone or is there someone who can accompany you to greet the buyer?

Generally, people who live in large cities have more reason to be concerned for their safety than those in towns or rural areas where people are well acquainted with one another. If you are worried about being attacked or having your car stolen, keep as much of the process under your control as you can.

Meet the prospective buyer in a well-lit commercially trafficked area rather than at your home. If possible, schedule meetings during daylight hours. And always take a friend with you to show your car. Make sure you ask for a valid driver's license before allowing anyone to test-drive your car. While you have the license in your hand, write down the prospective buyer's name, address, and license number. You can also insist that you go along on the test drive. Schedule your showings in close proximity to each other. You will not only be safer, but this technique also gives everyone the impression that your car is in demand.

In selling your car yourself, you not only want to protect your physical safety but also your money and your legal rights. When you trade your car in to a dealership, they print out receipts in triplicate for you and the Department of Motor Vehicles. But when you sell your car yourself, you are responsible for writing your own receipts.

Some stationery companies sell printed auto receipts with disclaimers on them so you are protected in the event the car fails to perform after the sale. Make sure you print legibly on every receipt the statement: "This car is sold *as is*. No warranty is given, explicit or implied." You must clearly convey to the buyer that you are not offering any warranty on the car once it is driven away. In addition, your receipt should include your name, the name of the buyer, the date of sale, and the year, make, and model of the car as well as its Vehicle Identification Number (VIN). Both parties should sign it.

Last, accept only cash or a certified check as payment. Do not take a personal check, no matter how well you think you know the buyer. And remember, it is not your concern how the individual finances the purchase so long as they present you with the full payment up front.

SALESMANSHIP

Remember my exposé of car sales tactics in chapter 3? They were intended to teach you to be a wary consumer, but now is the time to turn things around and put some of those tactics to work when selling your own car. First, take courteous control of your conversations with prospective buyers. At the outset you should ask callers for their names and numbers. If they refuse to give this information, they reveal that they are not serious about your car.

As part of your preparation, you should list all of your car's positive attributes. Is it a popular model? Does it have low mileage given its age? Were the miles you put on predominantly through highway driving? This kind of driving minimizes wear and tear on the car's mechanical systems. You should be able to rattle off to any caller your auto's positive attributes to show why it is worth what you are asking. Defend the price of your car!

Be prepared to discuss any of the car's negative points if asked. Tell the caller how pleased you have been with your car and how fortunate you have been to own it. Always be truthful, but emphasize the positive. Do your best to discover what the caller's needs are and try to sell your car as the solution to these needs.

One of the first questions that prospective buyers often ask is: "Why are you selling your car?" This is not a question I would ask a seller myself because as a salesman, I know that there are any number of ways to sugarcoat the answer. If you are tempted to say, "I'm sick of this thing dying at every stop sign on the way to work," take some time to work on a better answer ahead of time.

Callers also may ask: "What is wrong with the car?" You should honestly state what you know, but you shouldn't be expected to have the knowledge of a mechanic. You may fear that the "ping" you've been hearing is a sign of a major problem, but it might be minor and easily fixable. If buyers are serious, let them look under the hood or crawl under the car. They should also have their own mechanic inspect it. If you have any questions about how much you are legally obligated to disclose, refer to your state Attorney General's office or Department of Motor Vehicles. They may have a Web site documenting disclosure laws for private-party automobile sales.

Another question you should be ready for is: "How low are you willing to go on the price?" *Don't talk price on the phone.* Employ the old wisdom used effectively for many years by dealerships. Tell the caller that you are fielding many responses to your advertisement. Because other people are interested in looking at the car, you are not willing to talk price right now. You can let the caller know that you may be willing to negotiate on the price in person once he or she has seen the car.

PLAN AHEAD AND DO IT YOURSELF

Now that you know what selling your car really entails, let's remember why you should do it: to get the maximum money for your current car. No 100 percent sale or dealership gimmick is going to serve you as well as your own resourcefulness. With the proper research and preparation, you can make your current car pay for itself, giving you the most cash possible to put toward the purchase of a new car.

Your first job is to put just enough time and money into beautifying your car so that it makes a great first impression. If you've babied the car the whole time you've owned it, your efforts will now be rewarded. See chapter 11 to find out how to use the Internet to properly maintain and repair your car at the lowest prices. Even if you've let the car slide into disrepair, it can still fetch you more than you'd think.

Just make sure that when you are ready to sell, you give the car a thorough cleaning. Get rid of all the fast-food wrappers that have accumulated on the floor. Vacuum the carpeting and upholstery. Clean up any spots on the interior with spot remover. Stitch up any minor rips or tears. Air the car out, especially if you smoke. And treat the exterior to a wash-and-wax job. A little spot paint can do wonders on those slight scrapes and chips. Chrome polish can yield a luster that even the most skeptical observer can't help but notice.

 Is now the time to make any major repairs? Probably not. While you might correct obvious and inexpensive problems such as a worn hose or a blown fuse, you do not want to sink too much money into the car if you plan to sell it. Repairs are long-term investments whose costs are recouped over time as you get use out of the car. Your goal here is to give the impression that you've kept the car in good shape. Most people will conclude that if you've kept up its appearance, you've also maintained its inner workings.

Another preparatory step you should take if you financed your current car is contacting your financing institution to determine the payoff on your car. Once you learn how much you still owe, you must arrange to make that payoff to the lender. Only then will you be able to take title of the car and transfer it to the buyer. The worst situation you can be in is owing more on the car than anyone will pay you for it. If that happens you are considered by the industry as *upside down* or *in the bucket*.

You should also visit your state's Department of Motor Vehicles Web site if it has one. Chapter 14 lists state DMV Web sites (under the heading of "Government") that were online at the time of this writing. Your DMV can give you all the necessary information on how to transfer title, turn over sales tax, switch tags (license plates), and so on. Some states allow you to conduct the entire transaction at local tag offices.

PLACING INTERNET CLASSIFIED ADVERTISEMENTS

Why spend up to $60 a week for a small three-line advertisement in your local newspaper when you can place an ad for your car on the

Internet for free? Under the heading of "Classifieds" in chapter 14 you will find a sample of the many Internet sites that let you place free classified ads. In addition, your newspaper may produce an Internet version that offers free classified advertising.

If you have a digital camera, you can take a picture of your freshly scrubbed car and place it alongside your Net ad. More and more computer owners are discovering the "film-less" digital camera, which takes incredible high-resolution pictures that can be loaded onto your computer's hard drive and then uploaded to the Internet. You can also shoot a regular roll of film and have those pictures transferred to a CD-ROM by a photo-processing laboratory. Make sure that they use the standard formats for displaying pictures on the Web, either JPEG or GIF. If you have a flatbed scanner hooked up to your personal computer, you can scan your photos yourself and save them as JPEGs or GIFs. Or you can create a text-only advertisement. On the Web you are not charged by the word, so you can describe your car in full detail.

Your ad may be seen by thousands of prospective buyers and you pay nothing. Does all this sound too good to be true? There has to be a reason why all of these services are handed out with no apparent strings attached! There is. Many Web pages created for public use—whether by industry, government, or not-for-profit agencies—sell advertising on these pages by placing links to other Web sites. For example, Kelley Blue Book's informational Web site may sell ten or more links to other commercial Web sites like financial institutions, auto buying services, insurance companies, manufacturers, or parts stores. The Internet allows advertisers to directly target those people who have the most interest in their products by advertising on Web sites that relate to their business.

And now you can become an Internet seller as well as a consumer. Let's begin the process of selling your car on the Internet.

STEPS TO SELLING YOUR CAR ON THE INTERNET

The process of selling your car on the Internet is quick, easy, and best of all, free! First you need to find the *book value* of the car, then find out what the market asking price of the vehicle is in your geographic area. Finally, you can place your ad.

1. Use the Kelley Blue Book Web site (**www.kbb.com**) to *book out* your car (find the value of your car the same way the dealerships do) for standard regional pricing (see figure 8.1).

2. Look up the selling price for vehicles similar to your own in your area by visiting Auto Trader (**www.traderonline.com**), Classifieds2000 (**classifieds2000.com**), and your local newspaper's classified section if it is on the Web.

3. Place free ads on the Internet and sell your car for hundreds or thousands of dollars more than you would receive from a dealership.

Kelley Blue Book Site

Let's start by clicking on the Kelley Blue Book button at CyberWheels (**www.cyberwheels.com**) or by going directly to **www.kkb.com**. Kelley Blue Book is still the standard resource in the industry to determine used car values. Other reliable resources are listed in chapter 14.

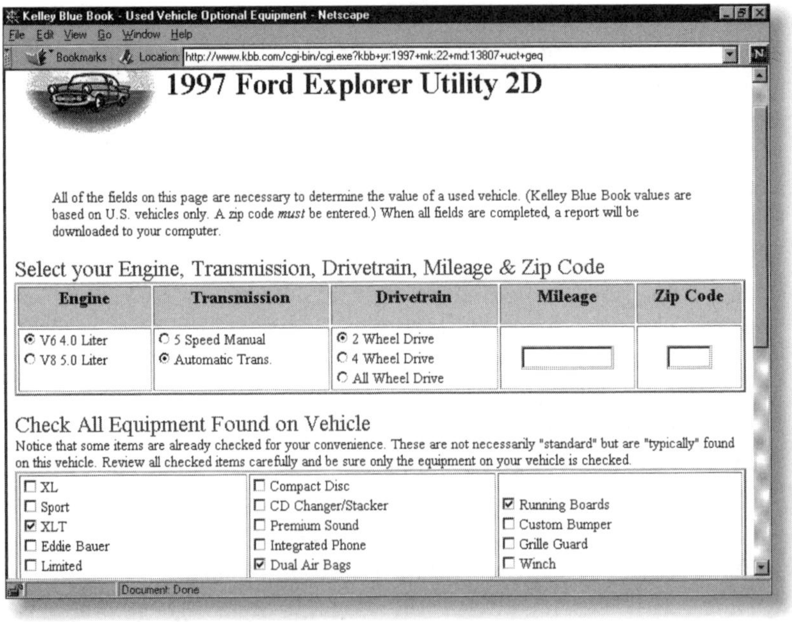

Figure 8.1 Kelley Blue Book [©1998 Kelley Blue Book. All rights reserved.]

Example: How much should we ask for a 1997 4-door Ford Explorer XLT, 2-wheel drive, in good condition, with air conditioning, am/fm stereo, dual air bags, and running boards?

STEP 1: Click on the *Used Car Values* icon
STEP 2: Click on *What's My Car Worth?*

On this page you will select the model of your vehicle, the model year, the options that your vehicle is equipped with, and the vehicle's mileage. You are also requested to submit your zip code to adjust for regional price differences, and the condition of your automobile. You can even get detailed explanations of what makes a car in excellent condition differ from one in good or fair condition. After you are done, click on the *Submit* button. For the example above, we listed only a few variables. You will be asked to provide additional information for your car, which will affect the blue book value.

The next page will show a recap of all of your data and a fair trade-in value for the automobile. For the Ford Explorer example listed above, the trade-in value we received for our zip code was approximately $17,500. Compare this number to the figures you get when you look up the actual asking prices for similar 1997 Ford Explorers in your area. This step is important, because no matter how accurate and up-to-date the price-guide sites are, they are not the ones putting down cash for real used vehicles. The bottom line is what people will pay for your car in your area at the time you want to sell it.

Local market conditions may boost your car's price a number of ways. If you happen to have a make and model that has become scarce in your area because of high demand, you might stand to receive more than a price-guide site estimate. Conversely, during a slump in new car sales, dealers are deprived of the trade-ins they need for their used car lots. Meanwhile people who are still buying are putting their money into good used cars rather than new ones.

Now we will compare the figures we received from Kelley Blue Book to real-life ads that are displayed on two Internet classifieds sites, Auto Trader and Classified 2000.

Auto Trader

STEP 1: Click on the *Auto Trader* (**www.traderonline.com**) link at CyberWheels

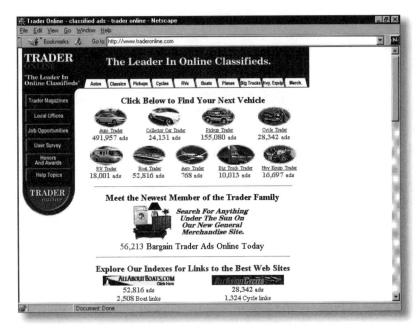

Figure 8.2 Auto Trader

The Auto Trader site (see figure 8.2) compiles a database of over 700,000 ads placed by private parties and dealers for cars, light trucks, pick-ups, vans, 4 × 4s, sports cars, collector cars—even RVs, boats, and heavy equipment. Think of all the trees being saved by the Internet! I like the idea of saving our timber resources and dump site space by using electronic media instead. Even in its present youthful stage of growth the World Wide Web already outperforms some traditional forms of print advertising.

Once you have arrived at the Auto Trader page, take a brief look at all of the categories and information it has to offer. This page is thoughtfully arranged to show tabs for various types of vehicles at the top of the page and related information and links to other Web sites along the left hand side. For consistency's sake we will be using the 1996 Ford Explorer as an example in this demonstration.

Before you go to the next page, take a look at all of the information that is available on this one: catalogs, financing, a listing of companies that specialize in parts and accessories, and much, much more! Later you may want to place a free ad of your own, but for now, we just want to find examples of 1997 Ford Explorers that are for sale in your area.

STEP 2: Click on the *Car Search* button on the side of the Web page

STEP 3: Type in the search information that is requested

The *Car Search* page will request your area code, the year range of the target car, the price range, and any key words you might use to describe the vehicle. Note that you have a choice between requesting area codes, states, provinces, or regions. After you have finished inputting this information, click on the *search* button.

STEP 4: View your results

You probably see quite a few examples of 1997 Ford Explorers to choose from. Reviewing these ads will give you an idea of what other people are asking for their vehicles in your area. In the examples that I found listed on the day I did this research, the asking prices for similar vehicles ranged from $18,000 to $20,000.

Take some time to look at how the ads are worded and whether they include photographs or not. Sellers can describe their vehicles

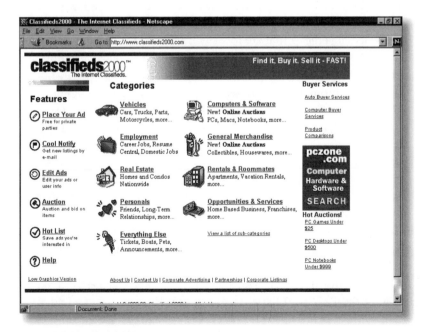

Figure 8.3 Classifieds2000

more fully on the Internet because they are not being charged by the word as they would be if they paid to advertise in newspapers.

Classifieds2000

STEP 1: Click on the *Classifieds2000* (**www.classifieds2000.com**) link at CyberWheels

Classifieds2000 boasts over 1.5 million listings. Before we move around this site, notice all the other fun areas that we can visit. This site has a unique Cool Notify feature for car buyers that sends an e-mail message when their desired type of vehicle is added to the classifieds. When you place your ad, a cool notification about your car may well land in the e-mailboxes of a crowd of eager buyers.

STEP 2: *Under Categories*, click on the *vehicles* button (see figure 8.3)
STEP 3: Click on the *Sport Utility/Jeeps* button

This will take us to an information request page. Enter your geographic location and supply the same information we used for the 1997 Ford Explorer XLT in the previous example. The result will be a list of all the actual vehicles that are for sale in the area requested, which will add to the arsenal of information you will need to make an informed decision about your asking price.

Browse through the ads to see how sellers phrase their sales pitches. When looking for cars similar to your own, you may even want to e-mail or call some of these advertisers to inquire whether they got their asking prices and how many responses they received from placing their ads on the Internet.

If you are still uncomfortable with the idea of selling your car privately, you now have a great deal of information to use at the dealership if you decide to use it as a trade-in when buying a new car. You can also shop your car around to used car lots. While it is unlikely that these places will give you much above the wholesale market value, you will be able to keep your dealer from stealing your trade.

Results of this search: The Kelley Blue Book site suggested that the value of the 1997 Ford Explorer is $17,500. The two classified ad Web sites listed similar vehicles selling for between $18,000 and $21,000. Now it's time to decide your asking price. If you are not in a rush, offer your vehicle high and incrementally drop the price each week until the vehicle is sold. Otherwise sell closer to the price recommended by Kelley Blue Book. The decision is up to you, but now you can make an educated determination.

Placing Your Ad

Your last Internet step is to go back to the Auto Trader and Classifieds2000 sites and place your ad. You will find their online instructions very easy to follow. You can also check out other classified Web sites listed in chapter 14. Use a search engine site such as Yahoo! (**www.yahoo.com**) to find out if your local newspaper offers free online classified advertising. You may want to go into an Internet chat room to ask for pointers from other people who sold their cars on the Web. Those sites are listed in the "Chat Rooms" section of chapter 14.

Don't forget the newsgroups devoted to online classified automotive advertising (e.g., **rec.autos.marketplace**) listed in the "Newsgroup" section of chapter 14. See chapter 11, "Internet Basics," for more information on how to subscribe to newsgroups that interest you. You can also check the Web site DejaNews (**www.dejanews.com**) to locate classified ad newsgroups that are restricted to your own geographic region. DejaNews has a search engine that will provide a list of local newsgroups based in your area (e.g., **la.forsale** allows people to post ads for all kinds of things in the Los Angeles area).

Once you've written an ad you're happy with and you've uploaded it along with a dazzling picture of your wheels, be ready for responses to come in quickly. Have your strategies worked out for dealing with potential customers, as detailed above.

A benefit to selling your car on the Internet is that fellow cyber-savvy people will feel comfortable buying from you. They will be able to pull a VIN report online at Carfax (**www.carfax.com**) to assure themselves that your car has no major accidents in its history. They may have even priced your car using the same price-guide sites that you used. The Internet provides an even playing field for buyer and seller to come together and conduct business in a mutually advantageous manner.

BOTTOM LINE You can make thousands of dollars more by selling your car yourself rather than using it as a trade-in. Using Internet price guide sites such as Kelley Blue Book and classified advertising sites such as Auto Trader and Classifieds2000, you can price your vehicle and then place a free online ad, bypassing the dealership *trade-in allowance* and pocketing the profit.

Chapter Nine

Good Credit/Bad Credit Internet Financing

> "A person who can't pay gets
> another person who can't pay
> to guarantee that he can pay.
> Like a person with two wooden
> legs getting another person with
> two wooden legs to guarantee
> that he has got two natural legs.
> It don't make either of them able
> to do a walking-match."
> —Charles Dickens

When I discuss the different aspects of car buying with people, I am surprised to find that while they are most intimidated by haggling over the price of the car, they find financing their auto purchase the least unpleasant part of the process. If they only knew how dealerships abuse the credit end of the transaction, they might consider car buying even more excruciating than they already do.

CASE STUDY: THE "NOT SO BAD" CREDIT

John Hernandez finally found his perfect dream truck, a black Chevy Tahoe. He had a very successful plastics manufacturing business but he had some credit skeletons in his closet. When his business was in its infancy, there were months when his credit was stressed and he and his wife had problems paying their bills on time. He had a Sears account that went into collection and his wife had a medical bill that was not covered by his insurance.

John knew that these problems would remain on his credit history to haunt him for many years, making it difficult for him to purchase a new car. Finally, after four long years of rebuilding his credit, he got up his nerve to go into a Chevrolet dealership to buy the Tahoe.

When John sat down to talk to the finance manager, he had cement in his stomach. Scanning the printout, the manager ticked off every blemish on his credit report. Then, pausing to gaze sympathetically at John, the manager said, "You've had some tough breaks, haven't you?"

John's eyes rested on his shoes as he nodded sullenly.

The manager continued, "Well, you've made an admirable recovery and I'm sure that if I talk to my boss, somehow we'll find a way to get you a loan." When the finance manager returned, he carried a loan contract and a smile. "It took some doing, but we convinced the finance company to float you the loan. We vouched for your character, John, so I hope you don't let us down."

John Hernandez quickly signed the contract, consigning himself to an interest rate of 22 percent. He felt obliged to the dealership for taking his case to the lender for approval. It was a remarkable act of faith on their part.

Hello?

After eight chapters of baring the deep dark soul of the retail car industry, have I finally uncovered its true humanitarianism? The dealership no doubt sought to paint its gesture in the light of beneficent charity, but let's analyze the facts of this case to get the real story.

Over the course of four years, John and his wife worked their way up until their manufacturing business was highly profitable. They carefully reestablished their credit during this time, paying off all of their delinquent accounts and never missing a payment on any of their new accounts. It is obvious to anyone looking at this couple's credit history that they overcame a common problem associated with many start-up companies and that they had nearly eliminated their credit risk.

Most financial institutions would draw the same conclusion. These businesses are eager to lend money to trustworthy borrowers who can demonstrate their current ability to repay the loan. Had John Hernandez gone directly to a lender, he would have easily qualified for the lowest interest rate available on the market.

Dealers know how to assess a buyer's credit risk. They also know that many buyers cannot judge their own credit rating objectively. When John Hernandez expressed his heartfelt remorse for his past credit problem, the dealership reinforced his misconceptions in order to appear to be his financial savior.

John was grateful to sign for a truck loan with an interest rate of 22 percent but he should have been outraged. The dealership was able to pocket a good chunk of that interest according to its deal with the finance company that issued the loan. Meanwhile John wound up spending thousands of dollars more for his truck than he should have.

Unfortunately this is not an exceptional case. Because John Hernandez had no idea of the dealership's agreement with the bank, he was left out of the credit process completely. If he had spent a few short minutes checking bank rates on the Internet, his debt on his five-year truck loan would have been significantly lower.

WHAT YOU DON'T KNOW CAN HURT YOU

 The credit side of car buying seems innocuous to the consumer, but as I discussed in chapter 7, when dealerships *build the reserve* they get commissions (or kickbacks) from banks and other lending institutions. These commissions reward dealerships for the amount they can charge customers over the financial institution's base interest rates for car loans and leases.

In most cases, interest rates are enormously negotiable. The amount a customer pays over the course of the loan may increase by thousands of dollars when high rates are inserted into the final contract. Dealerships can find just about any excuse to raise the purchaser's interest rate, including the smallest blemish on a credit report. If someone has ever been more than thirty days behind on a credit payment, he or she is considered a *slow pay* and is penalized.

If a buyer's credit history has serious problems, even from the remote past, dealerships will take full advantage. The individual who has had something repossessed, had an account turned over to a collection agency, or declared bankruptcy is putty in the hands of skillful car salespeople. No matter how many years of sterling credit followed the lapse, dealers will see only the mistake because it can be turned into profit.

Even consumers with spotless credit records have an overriding reason to go outside of a dealership when seeking automotive financing—to eliminate the middleman. The very same lending institution that the dealership uses will offer a lower rate if you visit it directly because you avoid paying for the dealership's commission. Credit unions and banks have long offered alternatives to dealership financing. Now the Internet has multiplied your options and it is absolutely foolhardy to ignore them.

KNOW YOUR CREDIT RATING

If you're not sure what state your credit is in, you would be wise to order copies of your credit reports before you start car shopping. Dealerships smell fear, and no fear reeks as much as the fear of being shamefully exposed as a bad credit risk. A few credit agencies wield enormous power by tracking consumers' financial transactions in detail and judging who among us is creditworthy. The three major credit agencies—Equifax (**www.equifax.com**), TransUnion (**www.transunion. com**), and Experian (formerly TRW) (**www.experian.com**)—each have Web sites where you can either order your report online or find instructions on how to order a copy by mail or phone. There is a nominal fee for this service (approximately eight dollars; the fee varies by state), but

Figure 9.1 Equifax [©1998 Equifax Inc., Altlanta, Georgia.]

it is a good investment, especially before making a major auto purchase. If you have recently been denied credit, you can receive a report free of charge.

Even if you don't think you have any black marks against you, it pays to get your report just to make sure that all the information is accurate. You'd be surprised at how many incorrect items appear on people's reports, causing their credit ratings to suffer. If you've ever had a credit card stolen, the thief may have left your credit in ruins. Legitimate negative information that is over seven years old should be expunged from your credit history. You must take action immediately to correct any mistakes you find or they will hound you for a long time to come.

Your credit rating isn't solely determined by your past payment history. Lenders will also evaluate your debt-to-income ratio to determine your ability to repay a loan. You can use the Internet to figure out your creditworthiness the way the lenders do it. Go back to our home page CyberWheels (**www.cyberwheels.com**) and click on the *Debt-to-Income Ratio* Calculator button. This will take us to one of over fifty sites on the Web that offer calculators to help consumers see themselves the way

PNC BANK LOAN CENTER
Take Four Steps To A Speedy Loan

Debt-To-Income Ratio Calculator
How much of your income goes to credit payments? Simply fill in the worksheet below...

Payments to:	Sample	Yours
Mortgage	$520	
Store Credit Cards	100	
Bank Credit Cards	40	
Cars	185	
Student Loans	50	
Other Monthly Loans	85	
Total Monthly Debt	$980	
Gross Monthly Salary:	$3,000	
Debt-to-Income Ratio	0.33 (33%)	

Figure 9.2 PNC Bank's Debt-to-Income Ratio Calculator

potential lenders do—in this case, PNC Bank's calculator (**www. pncbank.com/personalfinance/products/consumerloan/4steps/ income_ratio_calc.html**).

Figure 9.2 shows PNC Bank's "Debt-to-Income Ratio Calculator" page. This calculator will approximate a figure that lenders consider very important: a measure of how much of your monthly income is devoted to paying off debt obligations. Fill in the box for your mortgage or rent. Add your average monthly payments for credit cards, auto loans, student loans, and other loans you are paying off. Key in your monthly salary, click on the *Calculate* key, and bingo! You have discovered your debt-to-income ratio.

Print out this page and let's go back to CyberWheels and click on the *Borrowing Power Calculator* button.

Figure 9.3 shows PNC Bank's "Borrowing Power Calculator" (**www.pncbank.com/personalfinance/products/consumerloan/4steps/ power_calc.html**), which requires you to input your debt-to-income ratio. When you are through adding the information requested, click

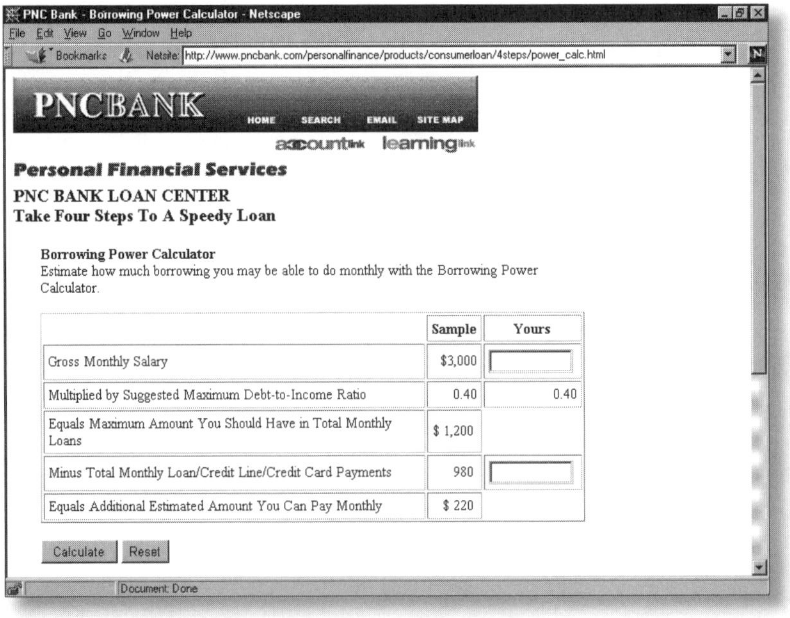

Figure 9.3 PNC Bank's Borrowing Power Calculator

on the *Calculate* key and the calculator will let you know how much money banks are most likely to lend you for an auto loan.

Armed with this estimate, you can figure out how much available cash you have to buy a car. Simply add to the loan estimate whatever cash reserve you can afford to spend and the fair market value of your current car as discussed in chapter 8 (minus the remaining payoff if you financed it). Now you have a ballpark figure when you go car shopping, so you'll know what is within your grasp and what is only in your dreams.

FIRST AID FOR BAD CREDIT

When you are in the car business you have heard it all. "My credit is bad because . . . I got a divorce, my medical bills were not covered by my insurance company, I lost my job, the collection accounts on my bureau belong to someone else, I bought a used car that was a lemon and I could not afford to pay the repairs, my mother-in-law nearly gave me a mental breakdown, there was a death in the family, El Niño . . ."

Some of these reasons are foolish and others are very legitimate. The banks know this and will request an explanation for credit blemishes before approving your application. They will likely look favorably on your application if your credit history follows this pattern: "My credit was good at the beginning and all my bills were paid on time. Then there was a situation in my life that was out of my control and I was not able to pay my bills. Since then, I have contacted the creditors where I was delinquent and have made arrangements for payment. All my other bills are current." If this is your scenario, you are likely to get a loan with a low interest rate. If you do not fall into this pattern, there is still hope for a car loan if you shop around on the Internet for competitive high interest rates. However, be careful not to fall prey to hucksters that will try to commit you to an interest rate of 25 percent or more.

TRUTH IN LENDING

The auto financing business has expanded and changed radically in recent years. For years banks have fallen over each other trying to woo dealerships to use their services. A common incentive banks use is a kickback called a *margin*. For every interest point the dealership can charge its customer over the bank's base rate, it receives a 30 to 40 percent kickback.

Dealerships make a killing whether a customer's credit is good or bad because they get the margin while the lender takes the risk that the loan might default. The higher a dealership can push the interest rate, the more it rakes in, even if the deal pushes a high-risk customer deeper into the very debt for which he is being penalized.

Now banks are falling all over each other to get on the Internet and seek your business directly. Lenders will now give you the same low base rates that they offer the dealerships. They will pre-approve you on a secure Web site before you walk into a dealership. To understand how to shop around for the best loan rates, you need to know the differences between the kinds of businesses that are ready and willing to lend you money.

LENDING INSTITUTIONS

There are three major kinds of lenders, and each is widely represented on the Internet. When I last checked, I found over 7,500 Internet lending sites. As you can see, the good 'ole capitalist system is alive and well.

It is not necessary to go through thousands of lending institutions to find the lowest rates but it's nice to know that they are all out there vying for your business. Once we look at the different types of lenders, I'll show you a site that compares rates within each state, giving you a quick and easy reference to make your decision. The three types of lenders are credit unions, banks, and finance companies or thrifts.

CREDIT UNIONS

Credit unions are the best place for a consumer to go to purchase a vehicle. They are not-for-profit financial institutions that pool the resources of members, who jointly own them. They typically offer a range of financial services, including auto loans, at discounted rates compared to commercial lending institutions. Whether you are financing a new or used vehicle, the rates are at least two points lower than those of the average bank and many points lower than what finance companies offer.

The catch is that you have to be a member of the sponsoring group (e.g. a union or a religious group) in order to qualify as member of its credit union. Rules have relaxed regarding qualifications to join, but the banking industry is lobbying to tighten the restrictions to keep more people from abandoning their higher-rate bank loans in favor of a credit union.

BANKS

Banks are for-profit financial institutions that offer a wide range of services, including auto loans. Unlike credit unions they do not require you to be a member to get a loan, but they may give better rates to customers who already use their other services, such as checking or savings accounts. In general, they base their loan interest rates on the customer's credit rating and on the number of months in the loan term. Their loan rates are usually a bit higher than those of credit unions but they are worth considering, as long as you go to them directly instead of through a dealership.

FINANCE COMPANIES

The last of the three lending institutions is a finance company. Unlike banks or credit unions, they do not depend on money from depositors to use for lending. Instead, they get their money from banks, other institutions, or money market sources.

Captive finance companies are wholly owned subsidiaries that exist to finance consumer purchases from their parent companies. The big three automotive manufacturers all have their own finance companies: General Motors has GMAC, Ford has FMCC, and Chrysler has Chrysler Credit. In general their rates are higher than those of credit unions or banks. Even worse, when you learn about these lenders through dealerships, you can be treated to elaborate song-and-dance acts from the finance managers instead of the numbers you need to compare financing packages from other sources.

Some finance companies exist to serve people with low income or poor credit histories. They authorize loans to people whose history might include repossessions, bankruptcies, charge-offs, collection accounts, garnishments, and liens. Banks and other lenders often reject these high-risk loan applicants.

These finance companies cover their risk by charging much higher interest rates than do credit unions or banks. Still, for those of you who might have no other recourse than to visit one of these institutions, rest assured that the Internet will help you comparison shop for the best rates among them. It always pays to apply elsewhere first and seek loans from these finance companies only as a last resort. Many people needlessly spend money on high-interest loans because they didn't realize they could qualify for a cheaper loan at a bank or credit union.

FINDING THE BEST RATES

Now we get to the heart of the matter: where to go on the Internet to get the lowest interest rate on your car loan. Let's take a look at a Web

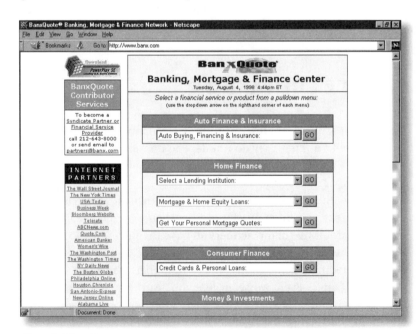

Figure 9.4 BanxQuote

site that provides nationwide comparison of bank auto loan rates. At **www.cyberwheels.com** click on the *Bank Rate* key. This will take you to BanxQuote (**www.banx.com**), shown in figure 9.4.

You will be prompted to click on the area of the country where you reside. The site will provide a list of banks within each state participating in this site's service. It will provide you with loan rates for new and used cars for different loan terms. Remember that companies shown on these sites may be paying for their right to be listed at that particular address. That's why I recommend that you compare the bank rates of a few different sites so that you will know that you are getting the best deal.

If you return to CyberWheels, you will notice that there is a *Search* button in the top right. Clicking this button takes you to the search engine InfoSeek (**www.infoseek.com**), where you can enter the phrase "auto loans" to search for commercial rates to compare. You will appreciate not having to run around town or go through the phone book looking for lenders. The best lender for you may not even be in your town, but halfway across the country.

After you have chosen your lender, completed their online application, and been approved, the bank will contact you by telephone or e-mail and offer you the following payment alternatives. They will either send you a check for the exact amount of the loan made out to the seller, a blank check that you will fill in at the time of contracting with the dealership or individual seller, or a letter of approval that you will submit to the seller at the time of contracting. The letter will give the seller detailed instructions on how to collect on the loan.

THE BEST RATES FOR HIGH-RISK BORROWERS

If your credit is less than spotless, you can still use the Internet to find the most competitive rates among lenders that specialize in borrowers with bad credit. I was visiting a dealership when I overheard a salesman tell a customer that the dealership's lender was his only hope for a car loan. This took place in California, where the usury laws are so liberal that dealerships can legally charge customers 29.9 percent interest.

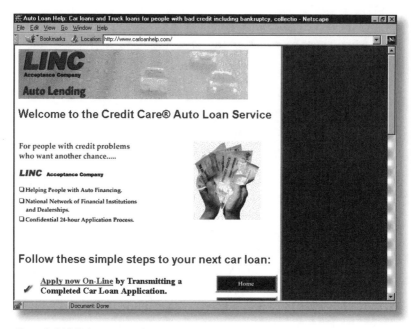

Figure 9.5 LINC Acceptance Company

While the salesman was very thorough in bringing up every one of the customer's past credit sins, for some reason he forgot to mention all the alternative sources of credit available to someone in the customer's position. Had the customer known enough to search the Internet for the best high-risk credit rates, he could have found rates as much as 50 percent lower than what he ended up paying. This translates into hundreds of dollars saved on monthly payments.

Figure 9.5 shows a Web site, LINC Acceptance Company (**www. carloanhelp.com**), that allows people with bad credit to compare dozens of bad-credit lenders across the nation. When you find the one that offers the most reasonable rates and terms, you will be able to transact the entire loan on the Internet. Wouldn't it be a great feeling to know that you have already obtained the lowest rate possible on your next auto loan before you call the dealership?

Also take note that you can obtain loans for used cars that are sold privately. There is no law requiring you to apply your car loan only to brand new cars sold by a dealership. As long as the lender is holding your collateral in the form of the car's pink slip it doesn't really matter where you got the car. LINC Acceptance Company is a great place to start looking for lenders that will fund poor credit risk "C or D paper." Browse through chapter 14 to find a list of other challenged credit lenders.

SUBVENTED RATES: ARE THEY REALLY WORTH IT?

Sometimes manufacturers will offer attractive auto loan interest rates to move their stock more quickly. They may even lower their rates far below the prime rate, which is the lowest rate that banks charge each other for loans. These *subvented* rates are advertised all over. You might have seen commercials claiming rates of 4.9 percent all the way down to 0 percent. Such bargains draw customers into dealerships in droves.

Despite all the hoopla, only a very small percentage of the public actually accepts these low-rate loans. Here's why: Manufacturers generally offer only short-term loans at these rates, which means you have to pay the entire principal plus interest over the course of 24 months rather than, say, 48 or 60 months. This translates into a monthly payment that is beyond the reach of most car buyers.

It's important to note, however, that manufacturers also offer a substantial rebate or other consumer incentives in lieu of the subvented loan rate. This is often the smart option because you can apply the rebate to reduce the principal on a loan you take out elsewhere, yielding lower monthly payments. Figuring out the math can be tricky but I'll show you the easy way to figure out what works best for you using the Internet. Boot up your computer and let's head out to **www. cyberwheels.com**. Click on the AutoSite link at CyberWheels (or go directly to **www.autosite.com**). Click on the *Loan/Lease Report* Button.

If you were offered a subvented interest rate for a new car of 4.9 percent for thirty-six months or a cash incentive of $1,200, which one would you take? Which offer would save you the most money? That is not an easy calculation unless you have an Internet calculator to do the work for you.

Let's assume the following facts and figures:

1. The total cost of the new car is $15,000.

2. The customer incentives are 4.9 percent interest for thirty-six months or $1,200 cash.

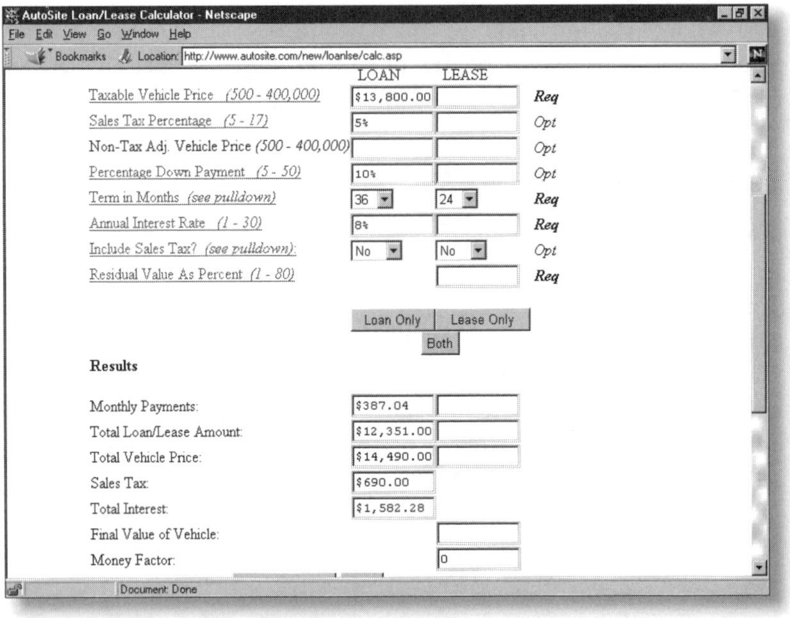

Figure 9.6 AutoSite Loan/Lease Calculator

3. The down payment is 10 percent.

4. The sales tax is 5 percent.

5. A competitive non-subvented interest rate is 8 percent.

Let's see what figures the AutoSite calculator provides and what they mean. Figure 9.6 shows what you get when you choose to receive the $1,200 rebate and apply it to a loan from a lender charging 8 percent APR (annual percentage rate). You can put the figures in yourself and click the *Loan Only* button to get the same results. We are most interested in the monthly payment, which comes out to $387.04. It is the number we'll compare against the subvented loan rate. If you pay this amount each month for thirty-six months, your total loan cost will be $13,933.44, of which $1,582.28 is interest.

In case you were wondering how AutoSite came up with the other figures, I'll go through the basic calculations. I subtracted the $1,200 rebate from the original $15,000 price of the car to get the taxable vehicle price of $13,800. That figure multiplied by the 5 percent sales tax yields $690. The taxable vehicle price plus sales tax equals the total vehicle cost of $14,490. I chose not to include the sales tax in the cal-

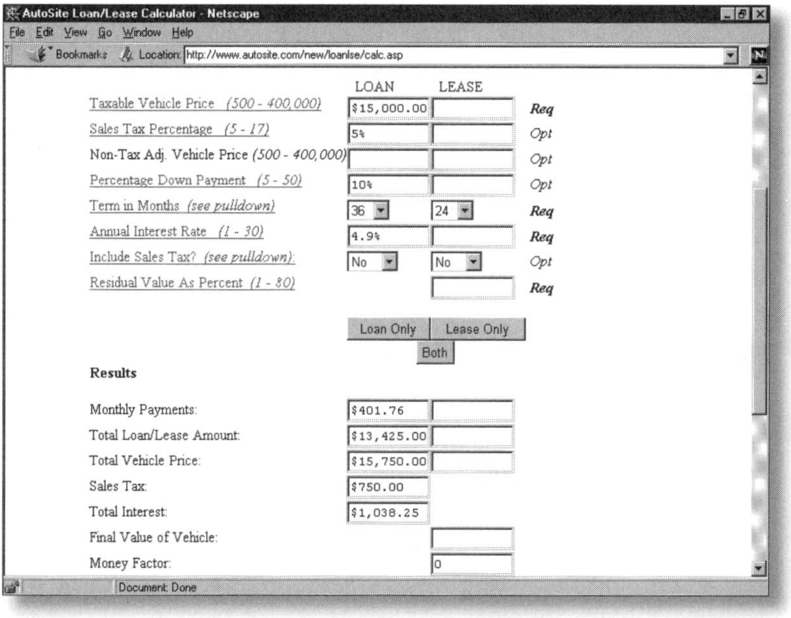

Figure 9.7 AutoSite example

culation of monthly payments because it usually is left out of those payments. Instead you may be asked to pay the sales tax up front.

The total loan amount was derived by subtracting the down payment plus tax from the taxable vehicle price. The down payment is 10 percent of the taxable vehicle price of $13,800, or $1,380. The tax on this down payment is 5 percent of $1,380, or $69. $1,380 plus $69 is $1449. $13,800 minus $1,449 equals $12,351.

Now let's compare this to the cost of the subvented interest rate. First print out a copy of the page for your records and then click on the *Clear* button to clear the page so that you can type in new figures.

Figure 9.7 shows the new car cost based on the subvented interest rate of 4.9 percent. In this case I input the full $15,000 as the taxable vehicle price. Sales tax of 5 percent on that amount is $750, which, when added to the taxable price, yields the total vehicle price of $15,750.

Again, the loan is calculated based on the vehicle price minus the 10 percent down payment and its sales tax, or $15,000 minus $1,575, which is $13,425. The monthly payments based on 4.9 percent interest over thirty-six months come out to $401.76. Your total loan cost would be $14,463.36.

According to the AutoSite calculator, you save $14.72 a month by taking the cash rebate over the subvented interest rate. Over thirty-six months, this adds up to $529.92. But what if you can't afford $387.04 a month, much less the $401.76? What can you do to lower your monthly payment? Try inputting a longer term for the loan, like forty-eight months, and see what happens. The monthly payments will drop. Unfortunately, lengthening the loan term is rarely an option for subvented loans.

REFINANCING

I bet you never thought about lowering your monthly auto loan payment by refinancing your present loan instead of trading in your vehicle. Many dealerships would like you to believe that the only way to get a lower payment is to get into another new car. When interest rates drop, you can first go to your present lender and request a lower interest rate or apply to other lenders for a lower rate. Very few car buyers ever even think about the great possibility of refinancing an auto loan. It's a great way to lower your monthly rate and the total cost of your present automobile.

You can use the Internet to calculate what various loans will cost you in monthly payments, figure out your creditworthiness, and find the lowest loan rates available for your credit status. You can obtain the loan online and have your financing in place before you even contact a dealership, sidestepping pressure and manipulation from the dealership's finance department.

Chapter Ten

Insurance and Safety

"Where no counsel is, the people
fall; but in the multitude of
counselors there is safety."
—Proverbs 11:14

People are alternately driven to seek novel experiences and retreat into the familiar. There is comfort in rehearsing certain routines and traditions, a sense of continuity with the past. However, we sometimes cling to habitual ways of doing things long after their utility is exhausted.

That is now the case with the world of conventional automotive retail insurance sales. Long known as an esoteric field full of actuarial tables, confusing terminology, and middlemen, it is now experiencing the Internet's mighty leveling effect. Those buyers who don't adapt to the Internet will continue to waste their money for the small comfort of having a "friend" down at the insurance agent's office. Those agents who stick to the tried-and-true will also be overtaken by the new breed of Internet entrepreneur vying to provide better service at lower cost.

Insurance is meant to protect us from the unplanned dangers that await us on the road. Optimally, we would never need to file a claim, because we would never get into an accident. We pay for a service that we hope we don't actually have to use. It is tempting to ignore the details of coverage as a gesture of optimism, but that would be a grave mistake. The wrong time to examine the fine print of your policy is after you have an accident. The right time is while you are still shopping for a policy. It even pays to consider your potential insurance rates when you are shopping for your next vehicle.

The Internet comes to your aid with a wealth of information about insurance. Because laws regulating auto insurance differ from state to state, you should try to find online information that pertains to your own state as well as articles that speak about insurance in general terms. You will find that most online rate comparison guides list rates on a state-by-state basis so that you can focus on those insurers that are legally licensed to issue policies to you.

This chapter will focus on getting background information about insurance, obtaining rate comparisons and quotes, and finally, finding safety information, including crash test results and recalls. The following sites may all be reached through CyberWheels (**www.cyberwheels. com**) or by going directly to their Web addresses.

GENERAL INSURANCE INFORMATION

A good site for background information is SafeTNet (**www.safetnet. com**). This site covers all kinds of insurance, including auto-related.

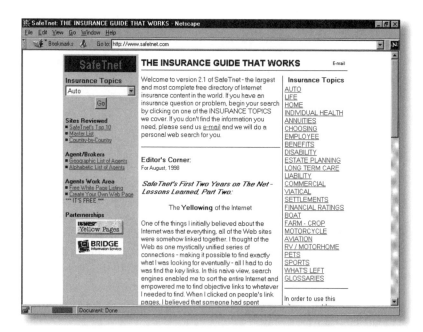

Figure 10.1 SafeTNet

From the home page, click on the *Auto* link to get to a version of the page shown in figure 10.1. It contains links to online articles discussing different types of automotive coverage (e.g. collision, comprehensive, liability, medical payments), uninsured and underinsured coverage, filing a claim, rate comparisons, lowering your premium, traffic laws and regulations, and much more. It also links you to information on theft, collision, and injury rates for different vehicle makes, models, and years. Because insurance is intertwined with safety issues the site also links you to information regarding alcohol, airbags, and other things that can affect your safety while driving.

Insurance News Network (**www.insure.com**) shown in figure 10.2, offers timely articles on a variety of insurance- and safety-related subjects. Here you will find the results of vehicle crash tests and other insurance issues of the day. From the column labeled *Site Index,* select *Auto* and you will be given a list of topics to choose from. Here are some intriguing questions this site answers: Where do you go if you have a complaint against your insurance company? How do insurance companies rate new cars? Which vehicles are most at risk to be stolen?

Figure 10.2 Insurance News Network

Which cars have the highest death rates associated with them and which have the lowest? Which cars have the best bumpers?

The Better Business Bureau (**www.bbb.org**) site in figure 10.3 is a "must visit" to get unbiased information about the auto insurance industry. It also answers a vast array of questions you might never have thought to ask about dealing with agents and insurance policies. This site also defines insurance terminology and lists the do's and don'ts after you have an accident. If you want to know your state's insurance pricing policy, just go to the BBB site and find out!

INSURANCE RATE COMPARISONS

Even if you are at high risk because of accidents or traffic violations you will be able to obtain free quotes as quickly and easily as clicking your mouse button. In the past it was a laborious effort to compare insurance company rates. You'd spend hours on the telephone repeating your

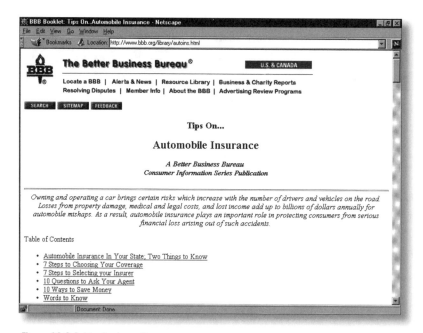

Figure 10.3 Better Business Bureau

information to a dozen or more agents. With the Internet it requires just a small investment of your time. Just click, click, click, and some rates will appear instantaneously. In other cases they will be sent to your e-mail address. Troupers who have fought and scratched to get the lowest rates may not believe how simple the chore is now.

Not only can you get the lowest insurance rates for your current vehicle on the Internet, but you also can determine which cars have the best safety record, which are at the highest risk for theft, and which qualify for the lowest rates before you decide on your next vehicle. By comparison shopping on the Net you can find insurance priced below the traditional market rates you would find through newspaper ads or phone quotes. A list of insurance brokers on the Internet is located in chapter 14. I'll take you through two examples here.

Before you power up your browser, gather all the information you will need to request a quote. In addition to your vehicle information and basic details like your age, occupation, and zip code, most sites will ask about your driving record, miles driven per year, and other driving

Figure 10.4 InsWeb

habits. You will have to provide details on past accidents and traffic violations. You will be asked to select the levels of coverage you want—it is helpful to have your current insurance policy handy to compare rates. If you are financing your vehicle, your lender may have specific requirements regarding your coverage.

InsWeb (**www.insweb.com**) in figure 10.4 provides an expanded listing of competitive auto insurance quotes just by clicking on its hot links. You can get instant online rate quotes from several insurance companies, including State Farm, AIG, Liberty Mutual, and Nationwide Insurance. Some insurers' quotes will be provided instantly, others will e-mail you or arrange for an agent to call you. The site also includes an Auto Coverage Analyzer that helps you judge if your level of coverage is adequate. In general, you want to have enough coverage to protect your assets if you are subject to a liability lawsuit as the result of an accident. The site offers comparison quotes not just for autos, but for motorcycles as well. It also has a link to Standard & Poor's rating of insurance companies as well as a glossary of insurance terms.

InsWeb makes it extremely easy to get an insurance quote. Click on the *Auto Quotes* icon and follow the instructions on the screen. In addition to the qualities of the vehicle itself, your lifestyle and demographic characteristics play a part when companies calculate rate quotes. Companies will target different niches within the overall market so that they offer very competitive rates to, say, thirty-year-old single males, but not to families headed by couples over fifty-five. Thus if you have been with one insurer for a while because its rates were once competitive for your lifestyle, you should check around for other companies that may better address your current needs.

In addition to sites that compare the rates that different companies offer, you can visit the sites of individual insurers. GEICO Direct (**www.geico.com**), shown in figure 10.5, has for many years eliminated the middleman by selling its policies directly to consumers over the phone. This company was already primed to use the Internet to broaden its direct marketing to consumers and pass the savings on to you. Other insurance companies that have a solid Internet presence include State Farm (**www.statefarm.com**) and Allstate (**www.allstate.com**). You should look for those that are willing to give an exact quote for the level of coverage you desire in your location. You can print out that quote and use it when making comparisons online or bring it with you if you decide to visit an insurance agent in person.

Figure 10.5 GEICO

Check to see if these individual companies offer any rate discounts for being a good driver, a good student, or a mature (55+) driver. Other factors that may cut your rates include being accident free, renewing an existing policy, covering more than one car under a single policy, having antilock brakes, having four doors rather than two, having anti-theft protection, or having air bags. Taking driver safety courses may also qualify you for rate reductions.

HOW ABOUT SAFETY ISSUES?

If you knew that you could quickly determine the crash test results of the car you were about to buy, would you take the time? Of course you would. If you're a parent, you're especially concerned about child safety issues. You can find out this kind of information and other safety considerations at the National Highway Traffic Safety Administration (NHTSA) site at **www.nhtsa.dot.gov** (see figure 10.6). As I mentioned in chapter 4, the site has a complaint form to register a complaint about a

Figure 10.6 National Highway Traffic Safety Administration

vehicle. It also provides information about vehicle features that can increase your security as well as precautions people can take while driving. Use this site to study the safety record of a particular car you are planning to buy.

Sadly, some cars fail to meet the exacting safety standards required of them to be legally roadworthy. Often their defects go undetected until they are out on the road in the possession of unsuspecting drivers. When enough complaints come in about a particular make and model, a manufacturer may issue a voluntary *recall* or it may be forced by the government to recall the problematic vehicle.

Whether you are planning to buy a new or used car, find out what its track record is and if has been recalled. It just takes a moment if you know where to go. Click on the *Recall* link on the CyberWheels Web site, or go directly to this page at AutoSite (**www. autosite.com/library/nhtsa/recalls/recall.asp**) and find out immediately if there are any secrets about your car that you should know.

BOTTOM LINE You can use the Internet to get price comparisons on insurance rates within your state according to your demographic information and desired level of coverage. You can also maximize your safety by checking out sites that rank vehicles according to various safety measures.

Chapter Eleven

Repairing Your Car and
Buying Parts . . . Dirt Cheap

"We have not overthrown the
divine right of kings to fall down
for the divine right of experts."
    —Harold Macmillan

After you've gotten a great deal on the vehicle of your choice, don't stop using the Internet for your automotive needs. The Net has plenty of information to help you maintain your car, spot warning signs, get the most reliable repair service, and find cheap parts and accessories. While nearly every automobile manufacturer has an Internet presence, car repair shops and parts vendors have been slower to catch on to this exciting and flourishing trend. You may find that some of the Internet repair-shop locators listed in this book do not turn up a recommended shop near you, even though locating an Internet-savvy dealership was a breeze. As time goes by, more shops will convert to the Internet in order to satisfy the growing number of Internet customers.

Now let's get to the heart of the chapter: using the Web to gain control over your vehicle's maintenance and repairs. After touring the different kinds of sources available online, we'll conclude with a step-by-step strategy to use the Internet to diagnose your car's problem, locate and purchase the necessary replacement parts for the cheapest price, and take bids from competing repair shops to make the proper repairs using your parts. The sites mentioned below and similar ones are listed in chapter 14's sections "Parts" and "Service and Repairs."

PUT THE "PREVENTIVE" IN YOUR MAINTENANCE

If you have just bought a new car, you should be covered under the factory warranty for regular checkups, safety inspections, and oil changes for a specified period of time. That means it is up to you to remember to go back to your dealership's service department according to a set schedule that is usually listed in your owner's manual. The manufacturer pays and you benefit.

But you are not restricted to using the original dealership's service department for work covered under your car's warranty. Many repair shops honor manufacturer's warranties, but your dealership won't volunteer that information. They make good money doing warranty work and do not want to lose it to competing shops.

Once your basic service warranty has expired, you have to take care of routine upkeep to ensure the long life of your vehicle. The Internet has plenty of advice to help you do this. For a fee, a service called Mile Minder Express (**web.wt.net/~clbmmx/**) will send you regular reminders to perform routine maintenance on your vehicle. If you have trouble remembering to get your oil changed every three months or three thousand miles, you might want to invest in this helpful service. For the more self-sufficient, the public television show *MotorWeek* has a Web site (see figure 11.1) that includes a preventive maintenance schedule created by Pat Goss of Goss's Garage (**www.mpt.org/mpt/motorweek/mainlist.html**).

Providers of routine maintenance services are also on the Net, e.g., JiffyLube (**www.jiffylube.com**). The AutoVantage site (**www.cuc.com/ctg/cgi-bin/AutoSavings/**) offers a 10 to 20 percent discount from a variety of automotive service providers across the country. Those who sign up for AutoVantage membership may obtain coupons for free maintenance services from several national chains.

The Car Care Council (**www.peoplevision.com/carcare/**) dispenses maintenance and repair tips and car care news on their Web site. One article on their site, "Better Cars, Better Maintenance Combine for Better Environment," explains how a new air filter or some new spark plugs could reduce the emissions of many cars now on the road. Another set of environmentally friendly tips comes from the National Institute for Automotive Service Excellence (**www.asecert.org/tips/tips1.html**).

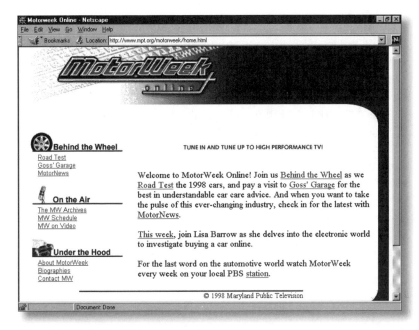

Figure 11.1 MotorWeek Online

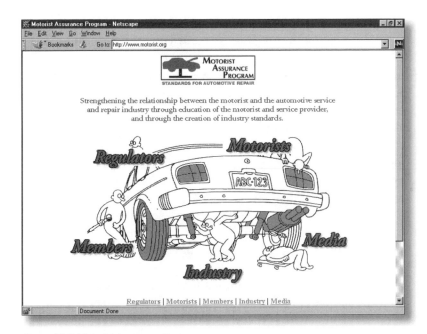

Figure 11.2 Motorist Assurance Program

Among the tips are getting your air conditioning system checked to avoid leaking CFCs into the atmosphere and keeping your tires properly inflated to optimize gas mileage. Another site focused on maintaining your car is Family Car: the Dream and the Reality (**www.familycar.com**).

For a site that gives thorough maintenance tips complete with clear illustrations, check out How to Find Your Way Under the Hood & Around the Car (**www.motorist.org/e1.htm**) from the Motorist Assurance Program (see figure 11.2). Cute little mechanics swarm all over the engine pointing out the battery, coolant system, and other parts for the novice while the text dispenses concise instructions on how to maintain the car.

For those with the curiosity to delve deeper into the mysteries of their vehicles, I suggest you study "Automotive 101" at AUTOSHOP-Online (**www.autoshop-online.com/auto101.html**). Each major system is explained with text and illustrations.

YOUR VEHICLE'S VITAL SIGNS

A number of sites go beyond giving routine maintenance information into the murky territory known as "stuff going wrong." The quicker you take note and take action, the lower the eventual cost will be. Must I retell the horror story of what happens when you forget about your motor oil until it all disappears and the entire engine seizes up? What about that *hmmmrrrruuummmmmrumm—kerchunk* sound you started to hear? What's serious and what's easily fixable?

A do-it-yourself auto diagnostic program is available from Meta-Cog called "Auto Tech for Windows." Check it out at **www.meta-cog.com**. There are also several Web sites devoted to automotive troubleshooting. AutoSite's "Garage" section (**www.autosite.com/garage/garmenu.asp**) has a well-organized set of hierarchical menus that let you select from a variety of symptoms you notice and then choose from a list of possible causes. For each cause you choose, you may learn more by selecting a Question & Answer format for basic information, a Repair Manual format for more advanced fix-it advice, or an automotive encyclopedia for in-depth technical coverage. We'll visit this site in our step-by-step exercise at the end of the chapter. An amateur Web site, Automotive Troubleshooting (**www2.uic.edu/~ msvest1/trouble.html**), has a similar hierarchical menu structure for diagnosing your car's woes.

You can also choose to have trained mechanics study a description of your car's symptoms and render a diagnosis for a fee. At AUTOSHOP-Online (**www.autoshop-online.com**), $29.95 will buy you a diagnosis of your problem. Describe it in detail and by the end of the following business day, one of AUTOSHOP's master technicians will e-mail you the straight facts. A similar service is provided by CarDocs (**www. cardocs.com**) for $16.95. These services arm you with professional opinions before you go into a repair shop. If you want lots of opinions for absolutely nothing, try subscribing to the newsgroup rec.autos.tech and post a message about your problem (see chapter 12 for instructions on accessing Internet newsgroups). If you are satisfied with the online diagnoses, you can purchase the necessary replacement parts yourself on the Web and save a bundle compared to what a shop would charge for the parts.

More help is out there for you do-it-yourselfers. The Gates Rubber Company teaches you how to detect a bad coolant hose at **www.gates.com/gates/squeeze.html**. It all depends on knowing how to grip it. And let's not forget that before there were computers, there was radio. Several car-related radio shows also have a presence on the Web, chock full of the advice they dispense to their listeners. Check out CarTalk.com (**www.cartalk.com**) to get the scoop from Click and Clack, the Tappit brothers, heard on National Public Radio. If you like Nutz & Boltz on the radio, check out Nutz & Boltz Online (**www.motorminute. com**). The Car Care Council site (**www.people vision.com/carcare/**) will lead you to the C.A.R. Radio Show.

Don't forget to keep abreast of manufacturers' recall notices. The National Highway Traffic Safety Administration (**www.nhtsa.dot.gov**) is the source of this information, but other sites, like ALLDATA (**www. alldata.com**), AutoSite (**www.autosite.com**), and CarPrices.com (**www.carprices.com**) also carry recall and safety defect notices.

Even if a vehicle is not subject to a recall, it may still wind up being a lemon. According to the Lemon Car Page's (**www.mindspring.com/ ~wf1**) article, "Sources of Applicable Law for Lemon Cars," *lemon laws* vary from state to state, but they usually conform to the following principles:

1. The statutes define lemon cars and require that manufacturers (not dealers) remedy the defects. Most statutes define "lemonness" in terms of a car that continues to have a defect that substantially impairs its use, value, or safety after a reasonable number of attempts to repair the car.

2. Most statutes set up a warranty rights period of either twelve to twenty-four months or 12,000 to 24,000 miles. The defects must occur sometime in this period.

3. Most of the statutes contain a four-prong yardstick for determining when a manufacturer has had a sufficient number of attempts to repair, entitling the consumer to a refund or a replacement. These are:

   a. If the defect is a serious safety defect involving brakes or steering, the manufacturer is granted one attempt to repair.

   b. If the defect is a safety defect not involving a serious safety defect, the manufacturer has two attempts to repair.

   c. For any other defect, the manufacturers are usually granted three or four chances to repair the same defect.

   d. If at any time the vehicle is in the shop for a cumulative total of thirty days in a one-year period, at least one of those days occurring in the first twelve months or 12,000 miles.

If any of the four prongs are satisfied, the consumer is generally granted the right to require repurchase or replacement of the vehicle.

If you believe according to the above criteria that you may have a lemon on your hands, you should visit a number of sites. In addition to the Lemon Car Page, try Autopedia's "Lemon Law Information and Sites" page (**www.autopedia.com/html/HotLinks_Lemon.html**) for links to forty-six states' lemon laws to learn your rights in your state. Another useful site is The Lemon Aid Stand (**www.pond.net/~delvis/ lemonaid.html**), with its many links and buying tips to avoid lemons. You might not suspect your car qualifies as a lemon until after several repair attempts fail to solve a problem. Therefore you should keep meticulous records and receipts of all work done on your car. In fact, it makes good sense to keep such records as a matter of course for both maintenance and repairs.

SERVICE WITH A SMILE

It pays to keep a pen and pad handy in your new car to write down anything that doesn't sound quite right—a squeak, a rattle—or doesn't feel right—a shimmy, or a pull to one side. If you've bought a new car, you will probably be going back to your dealer's service department to get maintenance and repair work done. Check to make sure how long the car's service adjustment warranty is in effect; many dealerships do not want to be bothered with holding the hand of nervous car owners for very long. Also remember that the dealership is not the only place that honors manufacturers' warranties. Look below for hints on choosing a shop.

As for more serious repairs under the basic warranty or the *powertrain* (also called *drivetrain*) *warranty,* by all means get your dealership to do this work as necessary. The problem with many dealerships is that warranty work does not pay as well as work for which they charge customers because the manufacturer pays them at a lower rate. So your car may be given lower priority than those of paying customers.

Sometimes your new car has a problem that is not covered under any specific warranty but if you take it to your dealer's service department they will fix it for free. Are they being nice? No. Chances are it's covered under a *secret warranty,* also called a *policy adjustment* or *goodwill service.* Here's how Edmund's describes a secret warranty in its Frequently Asked Questions (**www.edmunds.com/edweb/top40.html**):

> A secret warranty, actually called a technical service bulletin (TSB), is a notice that dealer service departments receive from manufacturers regarding potentially defective parts that are not covered by a recall or the basic warranty on the vehicle. The dealer is instructed to replace or repair these parts free of charge, but only if a customer complains about them or if a diagnosis for a problem finds that the part is the culprit. You can get a list of TSBs for your car by contacting the National Highway and Traffic Safety Administration (NHTSA) at **http://www.nhtsa.dot.gov** and conducting a search for the information.

ALLDATA's Automotive Repair Information Internet Site (**www.alldata.com**) also contains information on these technical service bulletins as well as a range of repair information.

If you could not resist buying a service contract or extended warranty from your dealer, check out the FTC's (Federal Trade Commission) online consumer brochure, "Auto Service Contracts," to learn your rights to getting work done on your vehicle under your contract (**www.ftc.gov/bcp/conline/pubs/autos/autoserv.htm**).

 But say you're on your own without a warranty when a problem occurs. How do you put the Internet to use in locating the right repair shop for you? Several sites have dealer-locator databases that you can search by inputting your zip code or city. For example, CarTalk.com has a "Mechan-X Files" locator that incorporates recommendations from happy customers (**cartalk.com/About/Garage/ intro.html**). The Family Car site has a locator as well (**www.familycar. com**). If you've been in an accident and need body work, Autobody Online has a Shop Finder database (**www.autobody-online.com/ shopfindhome.htm**). Be forewarned that these searchable databases may not turn up a repair shop in your vicinity. Even if they do, you should also check into the shop's reputation using the criteria that the FTC suggests.

A few more online avenues exist for finding a repair shop you can trust. You could subscribe to one or more of the newsgroups listed in chapter 14 and learn what others say about repair shops in your area. Those of you driving BMWs, Chryslers, Fords, Hondas, Jeeps, Mazdas, Mercedes, Saturns, and Volkswagens will be happy to know that newsgroups exist for your particular make of car. Antique cars, 4×4's, and custom cars also have groups of their own. And don't forget the chat rooms that I've mentioned before. You might find someone logged on who has great advice for you right when you need it. First, review the advice in chapter 4 about safety and privacy in cyberspace.

Another option is to use the search sites such as Infoseek (**www.infoseek.com**), Altavista (**www.altavista.digital.com**), or Yahoo! (**www.yahoo.com**) to look for Web sites that list and review repair shops just for a particular locality. Because this book is aimed at a national audience, I have refrained from listing too many sites that serve a narrow geographic area. I have included the existing sites for states' Departments of Motor Vehicles and a few localized sites if they also include general information. Consult a search engine to track down any site that might offer a repair shop database catering to your own area.

If none of these avenues turn up a recommended shop you can still find several places on the Net that offer good advice for finding the right place. Try the Federal Trade Commission's online brochure, "Taking the Scare Out of Auto Repair" (**www.ftc.gov/bcp/conline/ pubs/autos/autorpr.htm**). This handy fact sheet provides preventive maintenance tips and offers the following suggestions for identifying a quality shop:

1. Ask for recommendations from friends, family, and other people you trust. Look for an auto repair shop before you need one to avoid being rushed into a last-minute decision.

2. Shop around by telephone for the best deal, and compare warranty policies on repairs.

3. Ask to see current licenses if state or local law requires repair shops to be licensed or registered. Also, your state Attorney General's office or local consumer protection agency may know whether there is a record of complaints about a particular repair shop.

4. Make sure the shop will honor your vehicle's warranty.

5. Look for shops that display various certifications, like an Automotive Service Excellence seal. Certification indicates that some or all of the technicians meet basic standards of knowledge and competence in specific technical areas. Make sure the certifications are current, but remember that certification alone is no guarantee of good or honest work.

6. Ask if the technician or shop has experience working on the same make or model vehicle as yours.

Other sites giving similar advice include the Better Business Bureau's "Tips on Car Repairs" (**www.bbb.org/library/tipscar.html**), the Automotive Service Association (**www.asashop.org/docs/tips.htm**) and the National Institute for Automotive Service Excellence (ASE) (**www.asecert.org**), which awards the seals mentioned above. In addition to finding out what it takes to get their seal, the site has several tip sheets you can download, including one on finding a repair shop and communicating with technicians to make sure you are satisfied with their service. For example, they say that preparation is the key to good communication. You should be able to describe your car's symptoms clearly to a technician (or the person who writes up your order for the technician), including:

1. Unusual sounds, odors, drips, leaks, smoke, warning lights, gauge readings

2. Changes in acceleration, engine performance, gas mileage, fluid levels

3. Worn tires, belts, hoses

4. Problems in handling, braking, steering; vibrations

5. When the problem occurs: Is it constant or periodic? When the vehicle is cold or after the engine has warmed up? At all speeds? Only under acceleration? During braking? When shifting?

6. When the problem first started

This brochure tells you to ask any question you have no matter how naïve it might seem. If shop personnel use an unfamiliar term, ask for a definition. Find out up front what the shop charges for labor, what forms of payment it accepts, and what its guarantees are. AutoDigest's AutoJob (**autodigest.com/lookupf/job/job.html**) section can help you estimate how much labor goes into each repair. Its tips help you estimate what the shop should charge, whether it is using a flat rate or an hourly system.

And make sure to ask for an estimate in writing of the repair's cost before they actually embark on the work. If the repair will cost more than the initial estimate, have them call you to confirm before doing the repair. If the estimate sounds high, you may want to take the car to another shop for a second opinion. In this case, the first shop will charge you for the appraisal itself. You should also request to see the original damaged parts that the shop replaces.

And remember, you can go to the Better Business Bureau and the other consumer resource sites listed in chapter 14 if you need to lodge a complaint about a crooked outfit.

PARTS IS PARTS

You may find that you've learned so much from the Internet that you are ready to take on regular maintenance and repairs yourself that you once entrusted to the mechanics. Or you may become knowledgeable enough to diagnose your vehicle's problem but you'd rather let a repair shop actually do the work, especially if you lack the necessary tools. But if you can obtain the replacement parts for the repair, you could save yourself the shop's usual markup on parts.

You can use the Internet to obtain the best auto parts and accessories for the cheapest prices. The Net is home to a growing number of parts and accessories producers and distributors, so you can comparison shop and search for hard-to-find items. If you have an interest in antique autos or high-performance racing machines, there are plenty of sites for you as well. Even if you just want to learn what the heck motor oil really does—it's all available online.

 A remarkable aspect of the Internet is the massive number of people who took the time to put information on the Web as a community service just because they wish to share their expertise. Amateur enthusiasts have Web sites that stand beside the slickest commercial enterprises, often beating the pros in providing helpful advice to those who seek it. For example, if you want to find out what goes on inside those black boxes, car batteries, you will not be disappointed by the site, Sci.Electronics.Repair FAQ (**www.repairfaq.org**). You can likewise satisfy your curiosity about the wide world of motor oils by heading to More Than You Ever Wanted to Know About Motor Oil (**www.vger.rutgers. edu/~ravi/bike/pages/docs/oil.html**).

Beyond the Web sites are the newsgroups, where people argue vociferously about all manner of automotive minutiae. Find out more than you ever thought possible about auto parts by subscribing to **alt. auto.parts**. If you are in need of a certain hard-to-find part, advertise on the newsgroup **alt.auto.parts.wanted**. See chapter 12, "Internet Basics," for instructions on how to subscribe to Internet newsgroups.

There are many commercial Web sites to help you find the parts you need. A good tip for choosing a parts dealer is to seek a Web site headquartered outside your own state in order to save on sales tax. If you combine that savings with some of the discounts offered by certain sites, you can save some serious cash buying online instead of at a conventional retail establishment. Always make certain that the parts seller encrypts your transaction to protect your financial information.

General automotive parts vendors on the Internet include the wholesaler Auto Parts–WorldWide (**www.wwparts.com/home.cfm**), PartsVoice (**www.partsvoice.com**), East Coast Automotive (**www.**

ecautomotive.com), and the multilingual Virtual Auto Parts Store (**www.cruzio.com/~vaps/**). Even the venerable JC Whitney parts and accessories catalog is online (**jcwhitneyusa.com**). In addition, Internet search engines like Yahoo! (**www.yahoo.com/Business_and_Economy/ Companies/Automotive/Parts/index.html**) link you to hundreds of parts suppliers that have an online presence.

Some parts supply Web sites merely invite you to telephone them or request a catalog. Other sites permit online shopping. For example, the Virtual Auto Parts Store is one of many that asks you to fill out an online form giving your name, address, phone numbers, and e-mail address for them to contact you with a price quote. These forms also ask you to give very specific information about your vehicle before you get to the space to fill in what parts you want. Only give the information you feel comfortable providing. Many forms will still be processed if you do not fill them out completely. If you only give your e-mail address, you can be reached unobtrusively. Also, you may not want to give your vehicle's vehicle identification number (VIN), which is often requested.

Another way to go about searching for parts for your car is to check to see whether a local dealership that sells your model car has a Web site. More dealerships are advertising their service departments online, sometimes even offering discount coupons you can print out and use.

If you have specialized needs, they too can be met. For used parts, try A.C.S., America's Car Part Search (**autopartsused.com**). For antique car parts, check out Auto Parts Finder (**www.autopartsfinder.com**), AutoPro Collector Car Cyber-Center (**www.autopro.com**), Fomoco Obsolete (**www.voicenet.com/~fomoco**), or Kanter Auto Products (**www.kanter.com**).

Perhaps you're into high performance racing cars. Try Autobahn International Motorsports (**www.autobahnint.com**), Cyberspace Automotive Performance (**www.cyberauto.com**), Edelbrock Performance Products (**www.edelbrock.com/edelbrock.html**), or Lingenfelter Performance Engineering (**www.lingenfelter.com**).

If you're looking to customize your vehicle to express your personality instead of the manufacturer's, take a spin over to Autostyles Home Page (**www.autostyles.com**), California Dream (**california-dream. com**), or Sportwing, Inc. (**www.sportwing.com**). There are even sites specializing in particular makes, like MAZDATRIX for Mazda RX7 and

Rotary Engine Parts (**www.mazdatrix.com**) or vehicles from individual countries, like the British Parts Connection (**www.ultranet.com/ ~4british/**) or Germany's Van Essen Homepage (**www.noord.bart. nl/~essena/**).

And you shouldn't neglect the sites hosted by premiere parts and accessories manufacturers, which can offer valuable tips and information in addition to plugging their products. For instance, AC Delco provides a lesson in spotting counterfeits called "Beware of Bogus Parts" (**www.acdelco.com/parts/l1800.htm**). And Valvoline gives you tips on how to adjust your motor oil usage to accommodate different driving conditions (**www.valvoline.com**).

 You'll find several Web sites showing how to correctly use polishes and cleaners to maintain your car's exterior without wasting all that dough on dealer *protection packages*. Check out Duragloss Car Care Products (**www.spyder.net/duragloss**), Home and Auto Coating (**www.ef-polymers.com/homeauto.html**), Mothers Polishes (**www.mothers.com**), and Turtle Wax Home Page (**www.turtlewax.com**).

A STEP-BY-STEP GUIDE TO SAVING MONEY ON A REPAIR

 Let's go through the steps you might take to get the best rate on a repair of a typical automotive problem. Be forewarned that this endeavor is for those who are not intimidated by the inner workings of their vehicles. To save the most money, you have to use some elbow grease and diagnose your car's problem in order to buy your own parts. You may even need to invest in a few specialized tools to remove parts for inspection (these are also available for purchase online).

Step 1: Diagnosing the Problem
- From CyberWheels (**www.cyberwheels.com**), click on the AutoSite (**www.autosite.com**) link. Under the heading "Owning Your Car," click on the link for Maintenance and Repairs.
- In the "Troubleshooting Guide," you can select from a menu of symptom types: those you see, those you hear, those you feel, those you smell, starting problems, engine problems, braking

problems, transmission problems, steering and suspension problems, or tire problems. Click on one.

- This takes you to a page describing all the kinds of symptoms in that category. Scroll down to the symptom that best describes your problem.

- Clicking on the symptom brings you to a more thorough description of the symptom so that you can be sure it is really your car's problem. Then it gives probable causes. Clicking on any of these causes takes you to a page that gives you choices for obtaining information on how to confirm the cause and fix it.

- Clicking on any one of the causes usually brings up a page offering information in the form of Common Questions and Answers (the most basic), the Repair Manual (more advanced), or Auto Repair—Beyond the Basics (the encyclopedia at the site). It pays to select each of these in turn and print out the resulting articles. Note that articles in the Repair Manual include little camera *icons*. When you click on one of those, you see a straightforward illustration to accompany the subject being discussed.

- Try some of the other information sites mentioned above in "Your Vehicle's Vital Signs" or in chapter 14's "Service & Repairs" section to get more background information, if necessary.

- Here's the part where you must get your hands dirty and use the information provided to eliminate possible causes until one is left. This can become involved and may intimidate those who have neither the automotive background nor the tools to perform the recommended diagnostic procedures. If that's you, skip to Step 3, "Choosing a Repair Shop." Just reading about the possible causes for your problem will improve your ability to ask specific questions of potential service shops regarding repair costs.

Let's assume that you have zeroed in on the problem. You can check the AutoSite articles you printed out and other repair and troubleshooting sites mentioned in the chapter to identify what should be replaced in a typical repair of your problem.

Step 2: Obtaining Replacement Parts
The overall goal of this step is to find all the right parts at the best prices. Remember the general guidelines: Choose an out-of-state online vendor to save on sales tax and check each vendor for discounts. You

may choose from among the online parts supply stores listed in this chapter or in "Parts" in chapter 14. You may also use Yahoo! or another search engine to locate stores not mentioned in this book. Many store sites are really online billboards for their actual stores, which you must contact by telephone. Other sites allow online shopping and parts requests. It may be difficult to locate a site that actually places its full catalog of parts with prices online to browse through. Therefore, you may have to fill out an online request form and wait for price quotes to come back to you via e-mail or telephone.

Choose the supplier that gives you the lowest quote and only order the part online if they have encryption to secure the transaction. Otherwise telephone them to place your order. When you receive your parts, you can decide to install them yourself or you can go on to the next step.

Step 3: Choosing a Repair Shop

Before you track down repair shops, go to AutoDigest's AutoJob page (**www.autodigest.com**) and select your repair to get an estimation of how long it typically takes. It also tells you that repair shops often charge according to a standard flat rate based on one of several repair manuals: Chilton's, Mitchell, or the vehicle manufacturer's manual. You can then ask repair shops to estimate the time they expect to take and compare it to the AutoJob estimate.

- Follow the guidelines in the "Service with a Smile" section above to locate several repair shops in your area. Call them and explain that you have replacement parts and you'd like them to remove the old parts and replace them with the ones you've purchased. Obtain competing bids from each shop and choose the lowest price.

BOTTOM LINE There are Internet sites to help you maintain your vehicle, identify warning symptoms, find a reputable and reasonably priced repair shop, and shop for parts. To save the most money on a repair, diagnose your car's problem yourself using a diagnostic site such as AutoSite's "Garage," then order the necessary parts online to either install yourself or bring to a local repair shop.

Chapter Twelve

Internet Basics

"The difficulty lies, not in
the new ideas, but in escaping
from the old ones, which ramify,
for those brought up as most
of us have been, into every
corner of our minds."
—John Maynard Keynes

T his chapter is for anyone who has little or no experience with the Internet or even with computers in general. You do not need a computer of your own to access the Internet. We'll cover the basics of using Internet browsers on someone else's computer first, then discuss inexpensive television set-top boxes and other home computers you can buy, and finally tell you how to shop for a cheap *Internet service provider (ISP)*.

THE BASICS OF SURFING THE NET

Public libraries across the country are making Internet-connected computers available to their patrons. Call to see if your local library does and if it offers any training sessions on how to use the Internet. Public library Internet browsing is both free and easy. The software is already installed and running; you only have to come armed with the Web site addresses from this book that interest you. When you have a problem, you can ask the library staff.

If your local library is not equipped with the computers you need, try local colleges. Many allow visitors to use their facilities for free or for a nominal fee. You can also seek out a local café that is wired with Internet-connected computers. Most of these cyber-cafés charge a fee for the time you spend on the computer, so it pays to come prepared with the Web site addresses and other information you will need in order to find out what you want. But you get to sip a cappuccino while surfing.

Most Internet *browsers* make it pretty easy to navigate the Web. For advanced functions like installing *plug-ins* or customizing your options, refer to your browser's manual or online help file for instruction. For the purposes of this book, all you need to know is how to open a file. Move the mouse until the pointer is aimed at the *Open* button near the top of the screen and click on it. It will open a dialog box asking you for the location of the file you'd like to open.

You used to have to type in "**http://**" and then the Web site address that you wanted to visit, which began with "**www.**" Newer versions of Web browser programs now recognize addresses that begin with the *domain name* after the "**www.**" For example, typing "**http://www.edmunds.com**," "**www.edmunds.com**" or "**edmunds.com**" all take you to the same place.

Unfortunately, this general rule does not always work. Some Internet domains are given the same name as others, except for the "**www.**" For example, typing "**cyberwheels.com**" does not take you to our site, but to an Internet service provider. Therefore, always type in "**www.cyberwheels.com**" to get to CyberWheels. For this reason, the addresses in this book include the "**www.**" when it is part of the site address. If you do omit the "**www.**" when typing in the address you seek and the browser takes you to the wrong site, just try again with "**www.**" included. On America Online you can enter an Internet address in the *Keyword* box to go to any Web site, but you must type in the "**http://**" prefix, as well as the "**www.**" if applicable.

Another problem you may have is that some connections are slower than others. You may try to open a location only to wind up waiting several minutes for a response. You may believe that the address is not valid or that the site does not exist. But it may be that the site's server is temporarily unable to respond. Only when you get an error message saying that the address is invalid should you worry that the address is outdated (or that you entered it incorrectly).

After the site's home page pops up—which may take a while with a slow connection—you can scroll down by pointing to the down arrow in the lower right corner of the browser's window box and holding down the mouse button. Text that is highlighted in a color and underlined represents a *hyperlink*—a link to another Web page. That page may be part of the original Web site you are visiting or it may be part of a completely different site whose server could be located thousands of miles away from the original one. Whenever the computer displays information that interests you, print out the page by clicking on your browser's *Print* button.

When you want to return to a site you've been to, click on the **Back** button. If you wind up sitting and waiting for a Web page to load that is taking too long or isn't what you are interested in, just click on the *Stop* button to halt the browser in its tracks. If you need to search for a topic not covered in this book, type in the address of one of the Internet *search engine* sites, which will provide you with a list of sites containing the words or phrases you seek. These search engine sites include Yahoo! (**www.yahoo.com**), AltaVista (**www.altavista.digital. com**), Lycos (**www.lycos.com**), HotBot (**www.hotbot.com**), and Infoseek (**www.infoseek.com**).

You might be wondering how to collect data electronically from the Web sites you visit rather than print out everything as you see it. Most browser programs have a *Save As* command that lets you choose to save the Web page you are viewing as either a *text file* or as *source code*. Unfortunately, neither type of file preserves the look of the page you see on your screen.

Text files tend to jumble separate text columns together unless you select a monospaced font such as Courier or Monaco to view them with your word processor program. Source code files show you the *HyperText Markup Language (HTML)* programming commands that dictate how a screen will look. To anyone untrained in this computer language, HTML files look like a lot of gibberish. Saving HTML files can be useful if you want to save a list of site links that only appear in the browser's screen as text highlighted in color and underlined. The source file includes the actual *Web address* of each link if you look hard enough.

Another method is to take a "snapshot" of your screen using the appropriate keyboard commands for your computer operating system. For example, the Macintosh operating system lets you press Command + SHIFT + 3 to create a graphics file (in Mac's PICT graphic format) that can be viewed by its rudimentary editing program, SimpleText, as well as by many word processors and graphics programs. You can also obtain software that downloads all the files on a Web site that are linked together to form the text and graphic combinations of a particular page.

SOME WORDS ABOUT NEWSGROUPS

Newsgroups are forums for freewheeling discussions on particular topics. Unlike *chat rooms,* which allow real-time conversations among all who are logged on simultaneously, newsgroups are like an orderly bulletin board. Each subscriber to a particular group can post a message and all the messages appear in an organized list that is continually updated. Chapter 14 lists several auto-related newsgroups, which you can subscribe to through your browser program.

For example, under Netscape Navigator's *Options* menu, select *Mail and News Preferences*. This brings up a screen with several tabs across the top. Click on the *Servers* tab. In the box marked *News (NNTP) Server,* enter the Internet address of your ISP's newsgroup server. If you don't know what that is, call your ISP's technical support phone number.

Once you've done that, select *Netscape News* from Netscape's *Window* menu. Choose *Add Newsgroup* from the *File* menu and type in the name of the newsgroup you wish to subscribe to. Most browser programs allow you to customize the order in which the messages are listed. You can see them all in order of the time and date they were posted or you can see successive messages about a single topic collected into a "thread" before going on to the next topic. Threading messages helps preserve the flow of conversation.

On America Online, typing "Newsgroups" in the *Keyword* box brings you to an easy-to-follow forum for managing your newsgroups. If you know the name of the newsgroup you'd like to subscribe to, click on *Expert Add* and type in the name. Or choose *Add Newsgroups* to browse through a list of available categories. Once you've selected the newsgroups that interest you, click on *Read My Newsgroups* to view messages.

BUYING A SET-TOP INTERNET BOX OR HOME COMPUTER

A quick scan of the sales circulars in a recent Sunday newspaper shows that the most basic model of the *television set-top Internet box* from WebTV was selling for $99.99. You still have to pay a monthly connection fee to an Internet service provider to get an account, but this is a rock-bottom price. To make the best use of this book, you should also get a printer and a keyboard. These will add two to three hundred dollars to your hardware costs. The WebTV box comes with preinstalled software that is quite user-friendly.

Home computers keep getting more powerful even as they drop in price. Complete systems that include the necessary modem and printer are available for under $1,000. The Windows operating system is often preinstalled on these machines along with its resident browser software, Microsoft Internet Explorer. Comparable Apple Macintosh computers come similarly equipped. If the software is already installed, you only have to choose an Internet service provider and your ISP's connection information to have your own e-mail address and Internet account. You should also make sure the computer comes with as fast a modem as you can afford. A 28.8K (kilobytes per second) modem or higher is recommended.

 Helping you to decide on a computer purchase is obviously beyond the scope of this book, but the computer industry operates under extreme price competition. It pays to do some comparison shopping online at the library to help you decide what's right for you. One Web site that is invaluable is CNET Shopper.com (**www.shopper.com**), which provides a comparison price guide for all kinds of computer hardware and software. The lowest priced retailer is listed along with the contact information to place an order.

There are also free magazines like *Computer Currents* (**www. currents.net**), produced regionally with local advertising. *Computer Currents* covers numerous computing topics of interest to beginners as well as experienced users. Look for it in computer stores or sidewalk newspaper stands that carry free papers.

CHOOSING AN INTERNET SERVICE PROVIDER

Each issue of *Computer Currents* also includes a rotating list of Internet service providers available within the region each edition covers. In addition to its printed list, the magazine offers an ISP QuickQuote form to fax in for obtaining price quotes from various providers. This service is also available online from the magazine's Web site (**www. currents.net**).

Another online source of price comparison information on *Internet service providers* is The List (**www.TheList.com**). You enter your area code and other pertinent information and it returns to you a list of providers that meet your specifications. You may prefer a lower monthly rate for limited use (say, five hours per month) with an additional hourly fee beyond that, or you might want unlimited access for a higher all-inclusive rate.

You should consider not only the costs but also the reliability of the service. Some providers have expanded so rapidly that they cannot keep up with the demands of their subscribers. As a result, you may encounter frequent busy signals, technical difficulties, and service interruptions.

You also want a provider that keeps up with modem speed increases. As graphics and animation and sound files clog the electronic pipes of the Internet, the speedier your connection, the less time you'll spend waiting for files to download. If you buy a fast modem, you want to be sure that your Internet provider has local access numbers that can match its speed. It doesn't pay to have a 56K modem if your ISP only supports 28.8K.

If you become disenchanted with one Internet service provider, just remember that you can cancel your service and find a replacement with ease.

Another factor to consider is whether the provider requires you to sign a consent agreement giving it the right to inspect your private e-mail communication. According to the federal Electronic Communications Privacy Act, the provider can only view and disclose your private messages if you give this consent, so be wary of yielding your legal right to privacy.

Finally, don't be intimidated by all the technical jargon in the computer business. You should approach it as you do an automotive purchase: Comparison shop before making any commitment and never buy under sales pressure. Know the vendor's return policy before buying and check its reputation using one of the consumer resource Web sites mentioned in chapter 14.

Chapter Thirteen

Smile, Relax,
You Are Empowered

"Purchasing power is a
license to purchase power."
—Raoul Vaneigem

Wₑ live in a time where no single source matches the authority of the village elder, who was once the sole repository of the people's wisdom. Instead, a cacophony of voices competes for our attention and our trust. It is difficult to decide whom to believe when time-honored verities are continually cast away in favor of the latest craze. Is the Internet merely another in a long line of fads? Are we losing more than we gain in this headlong rush toward progress? In succumbing to the Internet, are we forsaking our ancient truths for glitzy new lies in a shiny technological package? Some decry the evils of the Internet, fearing it somehow dehumanizes us into preferring the glowing screens of our computers to each other's company.

But just what is so bad about that when it comes to business? If you approach the Internet with a dose of age-old common sense, you can use it to subject sales claims to the scrutiny they deserve. The *World Wide Web* has removed the physical and monetary barriers to comparison shopping. When a click of the mouse transports you from one site to the next, no tricks can trap you in any single cyber-store against your will.

Aggressive sales tactics work best when salespeople can use subtle facial, vocal, and bodily cues to overpower their prey. The Internet provides immunity against such intimidation. In its place is a wealth of choices without the pressure. You can explore possible purchases without being cornered by a store floorwalker out to boost commissions. You are able to take in all the information you need before making any commitments. Never again will you be coerced into making a purchase just to avoid appearing impolite.

People who long for the good old days of full-service sales forget how deception and greed drove much of those personal relationships between client and vendor. In fact, much of the automotive retail industry uses the veneer of friendship as a means of manipulating hapless customers. The message of the automotive retailer is *Trust me and you won't have to look for outside advice.* The industry does what it can to lull people into a false sense of security to make them dependent on salespeople.

In contrast, the Internet allows innovative businesses to try out new strategies to compete for customers. Rather than bid for customer loyalty through the old tricks of the trade, these new companies use the strength of the medium for organizing and presenting information. Whereas conventional dealerships put on a magic show full of illusions, the best Internet-based companies pull back the curtain to reveal the smoke and mirrors.

It is basic human nature to seek mastery over our lives. Empowerment is a gift we give ourselves. Too many people yield this essential gift to others, sacrificing self-determination for the promise of comfort or security. I have placed in your hands the essential tools to empower you to be a smart automotive consumer. Only you can use them to alter the balance of power between you and the sellers.

Previous books on car buying laid out laborious paths to empowerment. They taught consumers lacking access to manufacturer's invoices how to estimate a car's true cost to the dealer. They developed bargaining strategies that required multiple trips to competing dealerships, followed by several rounds of poker-faced negotiations on the final lot. The authors of those books steeled their readers to go into battle in full regalia because car buying was a fight to the death. Either you win or they win, but someone has to go down.

 This book shows that there is now a better way. Both parties can come out winners. Internet businesses seek more than your money; they seek your satisfaction. In doing so, they are transforming what once was a veiled adversarial relationship between buyer and seller into a collaborative one. And who wouldn't prefer collaboration to manipulation?

So now you can smile and relax because you have the tools to retain control of how you spend your automotive dollars. Now that you have completed this book, you can actually enjoy buying a new or used car, disposing of your trade-in, financing with either good or bad credit, and obtaining competitive leases, insurance, and warranties. Furthermore I have shown you how to diagnose your vehicle's problem before you bring it into the shop as well as how to find reliable repair services.

You can smile and relax because you are confident that you are paying the lowest prices possible. I have exposed all of the common dirty tricks of racism, sexism, and the hackneyed lies that dealerships have used as tools to get you hooked into the deal. I have explained the language and phrases of the opposition so that you will now be able to win this game with little or no effort. Information is power and the Internet allows us to utilize it to our greatest advantage.

Chapter Fourteen

The Best Auto Sites on the Net

"Knowledge is the most
democratic source of power."
—Alvin Toffler

Now that you've learned the ways you can use the Internet to satisfy all your automotive needs, here is a comprehensive guide to what I consider the best Web sites available. Given how quickly the Internet changes, I cannot guarantee that each site will remain in its current form, or even that it will still be accessible when you look for it. But the World Wide Web's explosive growth continually offers new sites to replace any that might disappear. I will continue to add useful sites and remove outdated addresses on my site, CyberWheels (**www.cyberwheels.com**). Be sure to keep returning to it for new information.

For space reasons I have omitted Web sites that only cover a small geographic location. Look under the "Search Sites" heading for Web sites that let you search the entire Internet for subjects of your choice.

Use all of these sites at your own risk. No single site has the final word; you should always comparison shop. You must combine skepticism with perseverance to become an informed Internet consumer. If you wish to protect your privacy, do not fill out online forms asking for such sensitive information as your name, address, telephone number, social security number, or financial information. For any online transaction, however, you must be prepared to give out the same information necessary when buying by phone or in person. To find out more about your consumer rights and the resources at your disposal on the Internet, see the sites under the heading "Consumer Resources."

Figure 14.1 CyberWheels

To make this chapter as useful to navigate as possible, I have organized the Web sites according to the following headings: Buying New Vehicles, Buying Used Vehicles, Chat Rooms, Classic Vehicles, Classifieds, Consumer Resources, Dealers, Financing, General Automotive Resources, Government, Insurance, Leasing, Manufacturers, Motorcycles, Newsgroups, Organizations, Parts & Accessories, Price Guides, Reviews, Search Sites, Selling Your Vehicle, Service & Repairs, Vehicle Identification Number (VIN) Reports, and Warranties. When a site contains information relevant to more than one of these headings, I've included it under each heading for your convenience.

BUYING NEW VEHICLES

Autobuyer (www.autobuyer.com)   You can buy a car online with this service. It locates a local dealer willing to sell you the car you desire with your desired options for only a few dollars over invoice price. You submit information about your trade-in car and the method of payment you choose.

Autobytel.com (www.autobytel.com)   The largest auto-buying service on the Internet. According to their homepage, over 1.5 million customers have used Autobytel.com's purchase request process. Their FasTrak service guides you through a simple, five-minute process for selecting and outfitting a new or used vehicle. One of Autobytel.com's 2,700 accredited dealers will contact you within twenty-four hours with a low price and delivery information. Do not use the FasTrak service to merely get price quotes because the participating dealerships expect requests from people who are serious about buying. You can also use the Bank Rate Monitor link to find the lowest interest rates in your state.

AutoConnect (www.autoconnect.net)   Search inventories of participating local dealers for the vehicle you want. Includes a calculator to estimate monthly payments and allows side-by-side comparison of statistics for up to three vehicles at a time.

Auto Connection (www.automart.com)   Allows you to search its database for new cars to buy or lease and then contact sellers by *e-mail*. Features for people interested in new cars include vehicle locator service and wholesale leasing.

Automall USA (www.automallusa.com)   This automobile search utility lists new cars available across the country. It provides dealer information and offers online ordering.

AutoSite (www.autosite.com)   Provides a wide range of information, including prices, service, and maintenance.

Auto SmartCat (www.autosmartcat.com)   This new car and truck buying and leasing service solicits dealers across the country to bid for your business.

AutoVantage (www.autovantage.com)   Information on the latest vehicle models and discounts offered by licensed dealers around the nation.

AutoWeb (www.autoweb.com)   Includes a new car showroom with extensive information and photos of one hundred new cars and trucks. Has links to price guides to show you competitive pricing. Allows you to submit a purchase order for the vehicle you choose.

CAP Automotive Information Server (www.cyberauto.com/info/)   Cyberspace Automotive Performance's site on car sales and leasing.

Car-List (www.car-list.com)   Includes new and used cars, has a calculator and dealer locator.

Cars@Cost (www.webcom.com/~carscost)   You can buy a new car through this service for $199 to $299 over factory invoice based on how long you are willing to wait.

CarWizard (carwizard.com)   This excellent site allows you to search its database of wholesale and retail prices for a wide range of vehicles and options packages, then find a dealer. It also includes important information on warranties, rebates, and car reviews.

Consumers Car Club (www.carclub.com)   Online buying service that offers retail and wholesale prices on new and used vehicles and connects you to participating dealers.

DealerNet (www.dealernet.com)   You can find photographs, specifications, and do a side-by-side comparison of vehicles. Obtain competitive price quotes from participating dealerships for the make and model of the vehicle you want. You then must contact the dealerships directly.

eAuto (www.eauto.com)   Has the eAuto-AutoVantage free carbuying service as well as insurance, financing, and leasing services.

Microsoft Carpoint (carpoint.msn.com)   Identify the vehicle you want, and Microsoft CarPoint returns a report with information on its specifications, safety features, competitors, and warranties. The pricing participating dealers offer tends to be MSRP, which is much higher than factory invoice. You can submit a purchase order and receive a local dealer's quote in several days. The site offers lots of multimedia glitz to show off vehicles.

Online Auto (www.onlineauto.com) This site offers new car buying and leasing and a dealer locator. Check out the great color photos of used cars for sale by dealers and private owners. This site also has a list of accessories, warranty information, and a seventy-two hour money back guarantee offered by many sellers.

Yahoo! Automotive Buyer's Services (www.yahoo.com/Business_ and_Economy/Companies/Automotive/Buyers_Services/index. html) Yahoo! provides links to over one hundred buyers' services and related sites.

BUYING USED VEHICLES

Autobytel.com (www.autobytel.com) This car buying site allows you to research pricing and model information on used vehicles, then use the Used Car CyberStore to buy a used car safely on the Web.

Auto Connection (www.automart.com) Allows you to search its database for used cars to buy or lease and then contact sellers by e-mail. Includes a used car evaluation service.

Automall USA (www.automallusa.com) This automobile search utility lists used cars for sale across the country and offers online ordering.

AUTOPEDIA (www.autopedia.com) This site features a systematic guide to what you should check out when buying a used car.

AutoWeb (www.autoweb.com) In addition to new car information, this site also allows you to search for a used car.

Car-List (www.car-list.com) A shopping service that offers good buys on used cars.

CarPrices.com (www.carprices.com) This site, in addition to giving used car prices, offers a used car buying service.

Cars.com (www.cars.com)   This informational site includes model reports, reviews, dealer locations, a loan/lease calculator, and consumer advice.

Consumers Car Club (www.carclub.com)   Online buying service that offers retail and wholesale prices on new and used vehicles and connects you to participating dealers.

Microsoft CarPoint (carpoint.msn.com)   Provides information about used car reliability.

Online Auto (www.onlineauto.com)   Allows you to search its database for the preowned vehicle of your choice according to make, model, and state.

Used Car Net (www.usedcars.com)   A searchable database of used vehicles.

World Wide Wheels (wwwheels.com)   Directory for used cars and trucks. Offers free ads.

CHAT ROOMS

In Internet chat rooms, you can participate in real-time online conversations with people who share your interest. You should be skeptical of what people tell you: They may have their own agendas or may base their opinions on limited experience. Commercial online services such as America Online (AOL) have their own chat rooms devoted to a wide array of subjects. The following are some chat rooms available on the Internet:

Auto On-Ramp (autoonramp.com)   This is a chat site with rooms devoted to general automotive discussions, auto racing, motorcycles, imports, classic cars, lowriders/custom cars, new cars, and car audio. It also has discussion boards where you can post a message for public viewing.

Auto Talk (www.autoweb.com/autotalk/)   At AutoWeb's chat room, you can share your ideas or ask for automotive advice from other users.

Consumers Car Club (www.carclub.com)   You can chat with a live Car Club operator if you have questions about any of its services.

eAuto (www.eauto.com)   Everything Automotive includes a chat room.

Edmund's (www.edmunds.com)   This site has a "Town Hall" chat room.

Yahoo Automotive Events (events.yahoo.com/Recreation/ Automotive/)   Links to the day's automotive chats and programs.

CLASSIC VEHICLES

Auburn Cord Duesenberg Museum (www.clearlake.com/ auburn/acd.htm)   Classic cars are on display in the museum and on the Web site.

AutoPro Collector Car Cyber-Center (www.autopro.com)   Online source of vintage, classic, and collector car parts.

Classic Auto Registry Service (www.kars.com)   In addition to having classified ads for vintage automobiles, this site lets you request a particular make and model and gets back to you within twenty-four hours.

Classic Car Source (www.classicar.com)   Sells online factory repair manuals, sales brochures, owner manuals, dealer product books for cars, trucks, and motorcycles dating back to the birth of the industry through the present.

The Dodge Dart Page (www.cyberbyteds.com/dart/dart.html)   Site devoted to the obsolete Dodge Dart (1963–1976), with images, information, and owner stories.

Fomoco Obsolete—home of Mustang, Ford, Mercury, Fairlane, Falcon (www.voicenet.com/~fomoco/)   This site is dedicated to 1963–1970 Ford vehicles.

Grim Rides Hearse Club (members.aol.com/hearseq/grimrides.htm)   The San Fransisco Bay Area has a club for hearse owners and this is its Web site. Plenty of creepy fun.

Hemmings Motor News (www.hmn.com)   This is the online version of the publication that provides a marketplace for antique, classic, vintage, muscle, street rod, and special interest autos. Includes many advertisements catering to car collectors, hobbyists, and restorers.

Henry Ford Museum & Greenfield Village (www.hfm.umd.umich. edu)   This online counterpart to the actual museum in Dearborn, Michigan, includes photos of such classic cars as GT-40 Mark IV and a 1931 Bugatti Royale Type 41 Cabriolet.

Indianapolis Motor Speedway Hall of Fame Museum (www. brickyard400.com/hof/index.html)   The virtual version of this real museum in Speedway, Indiana, is filled with Indy 500 winning cars.

Kanter Auto Products (www.kanter.com)   New mechanical auto parts for antique 1930–1986 American cars and trucks.

The Land Yacht Marina (www.voicenet.com/~perches/landycht. html)   A funny site devoted to the many full-sized gas-guzzling road monsters that have graced automotive history.

Motorsports Museum and Hall of Fame (www.mshf.com/index. html)   All kinds of motorized racing vehicles are included in both the real and Web versions of this museum in Novi, Michigan.

National Automotive and Truck Museum of the United States (www.clearlake.com/natmus/nat.htm)   For collectors. Includes a history of trucks and post-World War II cars. The museum is in Auburn, Indiana.

National Corvette Museum (www.ky.net/corvette)   Provides a Web brochure about the Bowling Green, Kentucky, museum devoted to Corvettes.

Petersen Automotive Museum (www.lam.mus.ca.us/petersen) This museum in Los Angeles has a virtual sampler of its treasures on the Web, including a 1939 French Delahaye V-12.

CLASSIFIEDS

AutoSite (www.autosite.com)   This site offers classified ads in addition to price reports and other information.

Auto Trader Online (www.traderonline.com/auto)   The online version of the print *Auto Trader* classified ad circular. It provides classified ads for used and new cars, lists car dealership inventories, and offers links to car manufacturer sites. It allows you to search for a vehicle by make, model, price range, and geographic region.

CarPrices (www.carprices.com)   This colorful site includes classifieds.

Classic Auto Registry Service (www.kars.com)   Classified ads for vintage automobiles.

Cars.com (www.cars.com)   Seven major newspaper companies teamed up to create this informational site, which includes used car listings as well as a loan/lease calculator, model reports, dealer locations, and consumer advice.

Classifieds2000 (classifieds2000.com)   Search the database for all kinds of vehicles, including not only cars and trucks, but motorcycles, vans, and RVs. Its "Cool Notify" service lets you input the specs of the vehicle you desire if you don't find it listed. When it becomes available they will e-mail you.

eAuto (www.eauto.com)   This "Everything Automotive" site includes the eAuto Classified Advertising Service.

Microsoft CarPoint (carpoint.msn.com)   Includes used car classifieds.

Online Auto (www.onlineauto.com)   Allows you to post your own classified ad to be added to their database.

World Wide Wheels (wwwheels.com)   This directory of used cars and trucks includes classified ads with photographs.

Yahoo! Automotive Classifieds (www.yahoo.com/Business_and_ Economy/Companies/Automotive/Classifieds/index.html)   Yahoo! offers links to classified ad sites for new and used vehicles of all types.

CONSUMER RESOURCES

Better Business Bureau (www.bbb.org)   The online version of the clearinghouse for information about the reputations of various businesses.

Center for Auto Safety (www.essential.org/cas)   This site founded by Ralph Nader provides the kind of consumer information he has long been known for.

Cybercop Precinct House (www.cybercops.org)   Not a legal authority but a group of private citizens—Internet Consumers' Action Network—that compiles information about complaints against online businesses.

Equifax (www.equifax.com)   Obtain a report on your credit history here.

Experian (www.experian.com)   Formerly known as TRW, Experian is one of the largest credit reporting agencies. Includes instructions on how to obtain a copy of your credit report.

FTC Consumer Brochures (www.webcom.com/~lewrose/ brochures.html)   Online versions of the Federal Trade Commission's consumer brochures.

The Lemon Aid Stand (www.pond.net/~delvis/lemonaid.html) This site includes tips on how to avoid buying lemons. It also contains links to government offices, consumer and lemon sites, and recall and safety defect information.

The Lemon Car Page (www.mindspring.com/~wf1/)   This recommended site offers such information as sources of applicable law, consumer strategies for lemon car cases, informal dispute resolution or arbitration, and a page of lemon links, lemon lawyers, and lemon reading materials.

Lemon Law Information and Sites (www.autopedia.com/html/ HotLinks_Lemon.html)   This section of Autopedia contains information about various states' lemon laws and includes links to related sites.

Online Scams (www.ftc.gov/bcp/scams01.htm)   A document that helps consumers identify the most common online scams and frauds.

Privacy Rights Clearinghouse (www.privacyrights.org)   A nonprofit group associated with the University of San Diego's Center for Public Interest Law that provides information on how to protect your privacy while conducting business, including online business. Its fact sheet no. 18, "Privacy in Cyberspace," is especially informative.

TransUnion (www.transunion.com)   One of the largest credit reporting agencies. Includes instructions on how to obtain a copy of your credit report.

U.S. Consumer Gateway (www.consumer.gov) This site combines information from a number of federal regulatory bodies, including the Federal Trade Commission, the Securities and Exchange Commission, the Consumer Product Safety Commission, the Food and Drug Administration, the National Highway and Traffic Safety Administration. It includes consumer alerts regarding cyber-fraud.

WebWatchDog (www.webwatchdog.com) An organization dedicated to distinguishing legitimate Internet businesses from those that have been put in the doghouse due to consumer complaints. You can search for a specific company or search by category.

DEALERS

Note that many manufacturer sites also offer a dealer locator service for their own vehicles.

Auto Dealer Locator Service (www.adls.com) Locate dealerships according to manufacturer, city, and state.

DealerNet (www.dealernet.com) Includes links to over seven hundred dealers across the country and a guide to dealers with unusual vehicles.

Internet AutoSource (www.autosource-usa.com) Provides information and photos of almost every manufacturer's model line. You can also locate dealers and get information on auto shows.

FINANCING

1-800-CARLOAN (www.carloan.com) This site promises to make every effort to find you a loan package even if you have bad credit. It represents a group of dealers nationwide, increasing the chances that your online loan application will be accepted by one of them.

Autobytel.com (www.autobytel.com)   This car buying site allows you to research finance options and apply for competitive financing after you submit a request to purchase a vehicle.

AutoSite (www.autosite.com)   Use the loan/lease calculator to determine what a loan will cost on a monthly basis.

AutoConnect AutoFinance (www.autoconnect.net)   The financing arm of the site's buying service will arrange a car loan within thirty minutes.

AutoWeb (www.autoweb.com)   This automotive buying service also has a financing service.

Banx Quote (www.banx.com)   Provides comparisons of different banks' lending rates.

CarFinance.com (www.CarFinance.com/fin/)   This site from NationsBank offers leases, loans, and refinancing on new and used vehicles. Online credit application available.

CarPrices.com (www.carprices.com)   Provides online financing in addition to information on car prices.

DealerNet (www.dealernet.com)   Allows you to check your credit rating or complete a GMAC financing application for $30.95.

GMAC Financial Services (www.gmacfs.com)   Provides automotive financing, leasing, and extended service contracts.

LeaseSource (www.leasesource.com)   Use this site's "Matchmaker" service to get credit approval within twenty-four hours.

LINC Acceptance Company (www.carloanhelp.com)   This site is dedicated to helping people with bad credit finance their next new or used car purchase. It has a nationwide directory of financial institutions and dealerships, as well as a confidential twenty-four-hour online application process.

PeopleFirst Finance (www.peoplefirst.com)   Provides secure, online auto loan products (car and truck loans) for established individuals with excellent credit.

PNC Bank (www.pncbank.com)   This large bank's excellent site has a "Personal Finance" section that provides calculators to figure out your income-to-debt ratio and your buying power.

Yahoo! Automotive Financing (www.yahoo.com/Business_and_ Economy/Companies/Automotive/Financing/index.html) Provides links to a variety of financing sites.

GENERAL AUTOMOTIVE RESOURCES

All Things Automotive Directory (www.autodirectory.com)   Has links to classic cars, classifieds, clubs, dealers, enthusiasts, finance, insurance, interactive sites, manufacturers, motorcycles, online magazines, organizations, government, parts, service, sales, and sports cars.

Autobooks.com (www.autobooks.com)   This site sells automotive videos, handbooks and manuals, posters, magazines, and model cars. It has secure online shopping. Every book is discounted 20 percent below list price.

The Auto Channel (www.theautochannel.com)   This multimedia extravanganza is full of sound and animation. You can hear *The Auto Channel* radio programs or find out about vehicles, parts and accessories, repair and maintenance, the auto industry, motor sports, and news.

Auto.com (auto.com)   Comprehensive daily auto industry-related news and reviews, including links to stock updates, racing news, forums, and breaking news.

AutoConnect (209.143.231.6)   Includes news and views, press releases, an online automotive bookstore, a vehicle search service, a dealer locator, a credit check, auto financing, information on vehicle affordability, and help with deciding whether to lease or loan. Allows for side-by-side comparisons of up to three vehicles.

Autoguide.Net (www.autoguide.net)   This is a large, well-organized site offering a wide range of automotive links. Use their online database to access voluntary manufacturer *secret warranties,* or *technical services bulletins (TSBs),* and the National Highway Traffic Safety Administration recall notices.

Auto-Links Trade Page—Web Sites of Interest to the Automobile Industry (www.findlinks.com/autolinks.html)   This site includes links to manufacturers, services, and suppliers in the auto trade.

AUTOPEDIA (www.autopedia.com)   The *auto*motive encyclo*pedia* is full of automotive-related information on such vehicles as cars, trucks, motorcycles, minivans, RVs, sport utilities, and even boats.

AutoSite (www.autosite.com)   This comprehensive site provides a wide range of information from prices to service and maintenance. It has up-to-date information on rebates and recalls.

Auto Town (www.autotown.com)   Offers information on new cars, used cars, financing at its "Auto Bank," parts, dealer locations, and employment.

AutoVantage (www.autovantage.com)   This car buying service includes information about buying new and used cars, selling your car, and maintenance. Most services associated with AutoVantage are free, but there is a $69.96 membership fee for its "Market" service, which provides a number of additional benefits. This site also offers cool 360-degree views of the interior of many new car models.

Bob Johnson's Auto Literature (www.classicar.com/vendors/ bobjautl/home.htm)   Sells factory repair manuals, sales brochures, owner manuals, dealer product books for cars, trucks, and motorcycles that date back to the birth of the industry through the present.

The Car Center (www.intellichoice.com)   IntelliChoice, Inc., provides information on automobile selection, purchase, and cost of ownership, including a list of the best overall values on new and used cars, and the lowest cost leases from auto manufacturers. Includes a helpful auto lease evaluation. For five dollars, Intellichoice offers a New Car Report that includes a five-year ownership cost rundown, complaint index, warranty information, rebates, dealer incentives, and more.

CarConnection (www.thecarconnection.com)   Provides news, reviews, and consumer information on leasing, buying, and maintenance. It also has links to a wide variety of automotive sites. Check out the *Digital Autobahn* link for the "baker's dozen" of their favorite sites.

CarInfo.com (carinfo.com)   Consumer advocate Mark Eskeldson provides tips on buying, leasing, and repairing cars and trucks, and discusses shady business practices and insider secrets.

CarPrices.com (www.carprices.com)   This site gives new car invoice prices, reviews, rebate information, used car prices, car financing quotes, car title checks, links to new and used car buying services, auto classifieds, car warranties, insurance quotes, insider tips, safety and recall information, and reliability ratings.

CarSmart (www.carsmart.com)   Has an Auto Advisor that provides information on many automotive topics, including safety tips, buying strategies, used car and service department tips. Check the list of dealer holdback and advertising charges.

Car Stuff (www.car-stuff.com)   Provides Web links for parts and accessories, magazines and publications, sales and guides, manufacturers, enthusiasts, clubs, electric and alternate fuels, associations, government, racing, auto shows, tools and equipment, museums, services, shops and stores, classified ads, and an information center. "Eddie's Auto Chat" through the *Services* link offers you an 800 number and, for ten dollars a call, you can talk to a real person to get professional automotive help.

CarWizard (carwizard.com)   An integrated site that provides price information on new vehicles, dealer locations, leasing, credit, insurance, warranties, reviews, and rebates.

DealerNet (www.dealernet.com) Has a search engine to help you decide which new and used vehicles best suit your needs.

eAuto (www.eauto.com) "Everything Automotive" has links to other automotive sites as well as news, reviews, car-buying service, and many other services.

Infoseek Automotive Channel (www.infoseek.com/Automotive/) This search engine site has subdirectories that link you to a wide range of automotive sites, including price guides, buyer's services, classifieds, financing and leasing companies, insurers, maintenance and repair sites, and parts suppliers.

Lycos Automotive Directory (www.lycos.com/autos/) This search engine site includes a subdirectory with links to the same range of automotive sites as Infoseek, plus it has a list of what its reviewers judged as the top 5 percent of all automotive sites according to their content and design.

Yahoo! Autos (autos.yahoo.com) You can browse new car information by make, class, or price as well as compare two cars, find a used car, get used car prices, talk about cars, learn about net auto events, get auto loan rates, find auto Web sites, find dealer locations, obtain industry news and use the yellow pages by inputting your zip code.

Zip-2 (www.zip2.com) The automotive section of this online yellow pages offers links to all kinds of services: auto brokers, auto dealers, car collectors, car clubs, parts and accessories vendors, insurers, and newspaper articles.

GOVERNMENT

A minority of states had Departments of Motor Vehicle Web sites when this book was prepared. If your state is not listed among them, go to one of the "Search Sites" listed below and search to see if yours has since created one.

Arizona Department of Transportation (www.dot.state.az.us/ MVD/mvd.htm) Offers online vehicle registrations, manuals, highway reports, and *Arizona Highways* magazine.

California Department of Motor Vehicles (www.dmv.ca.gov) Provides news, forms and information on special license plates, licensing, registration, codes, and new services.

Connecticut Department of Motor Vehicles (dmvct.org) Has records information, manuals, forms, and publications.

Federal Trade Commission (www.ftc.gov) This government agency is charged with enforcing fair trade laws and regulations and has many informational documents online to help consumers protect themselves against questionable business practices. The automotive industry and its advertisements are among the topics covered.

Florida Department of Highway Safety and Motor Vehicles (www.hsmv.state.fl.us) Includes information about driver's licenses, registration, and ownership of boats, cars, trucks, and recreational vehicles.

Idaho Superhighway: Division of Motor Vehicles (www.state.id. us/itd/dmv.htm) Has information on driver services, vehicle services, motor carrier services, and ports of entry.

IIHS: Traffic Laws & Enforcement (www.hwysafety.org/laws/ laws.htm) Summarizes various state laws on alcohol, drugs, motorcycle helmets, speed limits, restraints, and seat belts.

Illinois Department of Transportation (www.dot.state.il.us) Has announcements, information, press releases, road conditions, and safety resources for Illinois drivers.

Illinois State Tollway Authority (www.illinoistollway.com) *Frequently asked questions (FAQs)* about the state tollway system's rules. Also has maps and information about doing business online.

Massachusetts Registry of Motor Vehicles (www.magnet. state.ma.us/rmv/)   Includes forms, FAQs, branch hours, and other information.

National Highway Traffic Safety Administration (www.nhtsa. dot.gov) This extensive site within the Department of Transportation allows you to find out about crash test results, airbag safety, technical service bulletins, consumer complaints, and recalls.

New York State Department of Motor Vehicles Home (www. nydmv.state.ny.us)   Provides forms, brochures, custom plates, and other information.

Ohio Department of Public Safety—Bureau of Motor Vehicles (www.ohio.gov/odps/division/bmv/bmv.html)   This site offers forms, driver information, and special license plates.

Oregon DOT: Oregon Driver and Motor Vehicle Services Branch (www.odot.state.or.us/dmv/)   Gives state transportation, DMV, and safety law information.

State of Washington Department of Licensing (www.wa.gov/ dol/)   Has information on driver's licenses, titles and registration, fuel tax, and vehicle registration.

Texas Department of Transportation (www.dot.state.tx.us/ txdot.htm)   Provides information on licensing, safety, regulations, and highway conditions.

U.S. Consumer Gateway (www.consumer.gov)   This site combines information from a number of federal regulatory bodies, including the Federal Trade Commission, the Securities and Exchange Commission, the Consumer Product Safety Commission, the Food and Drug Administration, and the National Highway and Traffic Safety Administration. It includes consumer alerts regarding cyber-fraud.

Virginia Department of Motor Vehicles (www.dmv.state.va.us) Provides online transactions with the department.

INSURANCE

Autobytel.com (www.autobytel.com)   This car buying site also offers low-cost insurance quotes from the AIG insurance company.

CarPrices (www.carprices.com)   Provides insurance quotes from three hundred different companies.

Consumer Reports Auto Insurance Price Service (www. consumerinsure.org)   *Consumer Reports'* exclusive database produces a report of as many as twenty-five of the lowest-priced policies for your vehicle. Reports cost twelve dollars for the first vehicle, eight dollars for each additional.

Consumers Car Club (www.carclub.com)   This online buying service helps you get multiple insurance quotes to compare costs and coverage.

GEICO Direct (www.geico.com)   This insurer's home page gives a quick rate quote online, maintaining its tradition of cutting out the middleman by selling its policies directly to consumers rather than through agents.

Insurance News Network (www.insure.com)   This site covers many categories of insurance, giving information on such auto insurance topics as crash tests, industry news reports, premiums, minimum coverage, collision data, injury data, thefts by model/city, deaths by model, state information, State Farm and Allstate rates. It also provides an industry report card.

InsWeb (www.insweb.com)   This site covers several insurance categories, including auto insurance. Provides an "Auto Coverage Analyzer" to see if your level of coverage is adequate. Issues special reports on such topics as airbag safety and cellular phones. Also includes a link to Standard & Poor's rating of insurance companies. Has a glossary of insurance terms.

Progresssive (www.progressive.com)   At Progressive's site you can get an online quote for insurance along with comparison rates from up to three other insurers, including State Farm and Allstate.

SafeTNet (www.safetnet.com)   This site contains a wealth of links to insurance-related sites, including an area for autos. You can learn about different types of coverage, uninsured and underinsured coverage, filing a claim, rate comparisons, lowering your premium, traffic laws and regulations, and much more.

Yahoo! Automotive Insurance (www.yahoo.com/Business_and_ Economy/Companies/Financial_Services/Insurance/Automotive/ index.html)   Has links to many insurer sites.

LEASING

Automobile Leasing: The Art of the Deal (www.mindspring. com/~ahearn/lease/lease.html)   Summarizes all that leasing entails and estimates monthly payments to help you decide if leasing is right for you.

AutoSite (www.autosite.com)   Explains the advantages and disadvantages of leasing, defines leasing terms, and provides a loan/lease calculator to help you decide.

Auto Smartcat (www.autosmartcat.com)   New car and truck buying and leasing service that gets dealers to bid for your business.

CAP Automotive Information Server (www.cyberauto.com/info/) Cyberspace Automotive Performance's site on car sales and leasing.

The Car Center (www.intellichoice.com)   Announces best leasing deals (Gold Star Leases) available across the country each month. These are based on net interest rates compared across all evaluated leases and compared against the average bank loan or credit union rate.

CarWizard (carwizard.com)   This excellent site allows you to calculate leases for a wide range of vehicles and their options packages, then find a dealer. Use the "Lease Profiler" to see whether your preferences and habits are better suited to buying or leasing.

Consumers Car Club (www.carclub.com)   This online buying service offers a lease/loan calculator.

Golden Bear Auto Leasing (www.2leasecar.com)   Includes an explanation of leasing vs. loan terminology.

LeaseSource (www.leasesource.com)   Explains the intricacies of leasing, including terminology. The LeaseSource Wizard helps you calculate how good a deal you are getting on your lease. Its LeaseConnect service puts you in contact with independent leasing companies that specialize in locating and leasing new and used vehicles. Read the Leaseline articles in its Leasing Newsroom to keep up on industry developments.

The National Consumer Law Center (www.consumerlaw.org/ consumer/lease.html)   This nonprofit consumer law resource organization provides helpful advice on whether you should buy or lease, including information on the Federal Consumer Leasing Act.

Yahoo! Automotive Leasing (www.yahoo.com/Business_and_ Economy/Companies/Automotive/Financing/Leasing/index.html)   Lists links to sites with leasing information.

MANUFACTURERS

Audi (www.audi.com)   This product-oriented site gives information on five models, including a virtual view of the engine, maintenance plans, a dealer locator, Audi history, and leasing plans.

BMW of North America, Inc. (www.bmwusa.com)   Includes BMW dealership locations, news items and press releases, in-depth specifications for each model, and multimedia presentations. It includes information on certified pre-owned BMWs. Has a "Build Your Own" feature to customize the model you prefer, a "Speed Nav" section with many links, and a downloadable desk calendar.

Buick Home Page (www.buick.com)   You can design custom options packages for various models and obtain manufacturer's suggested retail prices (which do not include extra taxes and fees). The site includes a dealer locator and offers a "virtual reality test drive" of the Buick Riviera and other models.

The Official Cadillac Web Site (www.cadillac.com)   Allows you to select options packages for its models using the Interactive Design Studio, which includes a monthly payment estimator. The site also explains technical terms like Northstar System, and includes reference and historical materials. Information on Cadillac clubs and restoration of old models is also available.

The Chevy Spot (www.chevrolet.com)   Divided into the Car Spot, the Truck Spot, and the Geo Spot, with specifications, safety information, and pricing. Includes a monthly payment calculator and dealer locator.

Chrysler (www.chryslercars.com)   Includes specifications, pricing, special offers, and a dealer locator. Includes a "Tech Center" tour.

Ferrari (www.ferrari.it/ferrari/)   Global dealership information and beautiful racing photos in a stylishly designed site.

Ford (www.ford.com)   In addition to specifications and options packages, includes information on extended warranties, a dealer locator, the college graduate program, and the Ford Citibank credit card. Also has contests and an easy-to-navigate design.

Honda (www.honda.com)   Has Quicktime movies of its Honda CR-V sport utility vehicle as well as information about the rest of the Honda line.

Hyundai (www.hyundai.com)   Covers features of each Hyundai model and adds some Korean culture to the mix.

Isuzuville (www.isuzu.com)   You can order brochures, get Isuzu news, find information on each new model, and obtain information on leasing and buying.

Jaguar (www.jaguarvehicles.com)   A classy site that includes a model gallery, press releases, a dealer locator, financing and leasing information, and a historic library. It also offers a "Complimentary First Payment" deal worth $800.

Kia Home Page (www.kia.co.kr)   Highlights its concept cars, the Hybrid EV, and the KMX-3 as well as currently available models.

Automobili Lamborghini (home.lamborghini.com)   This is the official site of the Lamborghini company, covering the Lamborghini story, model photos and specs, Lamborghinis for sale globally, catalogue, news and events, and image gallery. Stylish design to complement its overpowering vehicles.

Land Rover (www.LandRover.com)   This site illustrates where you can go in a Land Rover in its "Adventures" section, which even reviews world-class hotels. Multimedia QuickTime movies and a screen saver are also available. Those who prefer straightforward information may be frustrated.

Lexus (www.lexususa.com)   Whimsically designed as the "Lexus Centre of Performance Art," which includes a model gallery, Dealer Grande Hall, Tech Centre, and Financial District.

Lotus (lotuscars.com)   The Lotus site includes information about its various models and accessories.

Mercedes-Benz (www.Mercedes-Net.com)   Includes vehicle information, an interactive map to locate dealers, and information about leasing, financing, and the Mercedes-Benz Mobility Package.

Mitsubishi Motors Corporation (www.Mitsubishi-Motors.co.jp) Allows visitors to view its extensive line of vehicles, including cars, trucks, buses, and RVs.

The New Dodge (www.4adodge.com)   Gives specifications on all new Dodge models. Highlights the Viper and includes the Skip Barber high-performance driving school. You can also order model kits.

Nissan Motors (www.nissanmotors.com)   Globally oriented multilingual site allows you to virtually look inside each model. Includes a dealer locator.

Pontiac Excitement on the Web (www.pontiac.com)
Information on the current model line, Pontiac history, and dealer locations. Includes a hypertext fictional road trip.

Saab (www.saabusa.com)   You can use this site to schedule a representative to bring a Saab to you for a test drive. It also has online information on current models and a dealer locator. You can take a virtual tour with the proper viewing software.

The Saturn Site (www.saturncars.com)   The Saturn site allows you to choose a model within a particular price range that you may buy at any Saturn retailer in the country. Also includes membership information about the Saturn CarClub. Has a link to the GM EV1 site about Saturn's electric vehicle.

Subaru Online (www.subaru.com)   Include model information on its entire line, including an explanation of the Subaru "boxer" engine.

@Toyota (www.toyota.com)   Photo bubble and QuickTime VR viewers let you explore the interior and exterior of Toyota vehicles. You can also order free brochures and CD-ROMs online.

Volkswagen (www.vw.com)   Includes an online dealer showroom that gives information about new models as well as a VW Museum covering the history of Volkswagens in the United States.

Volvo (www.volvocars.com)   Information on current models, their many safety features, and the economical overseas delivery option.

Yahoo! Automotive Manufacturers (www.yahoo.com/Business_ and_Economy/Companies/Automotive/Manufacturers/)   Links to auto manufacturer sites.

MOTORCYCLES

Classifieds2000 (classifieds2000.com)   Includes motorcycles in its automotive classified listings.

Motorcycle Online (www.motorcycle.com)   Billing itself as "The World's Largest and Most-Read Digital Motorcycle Magazine," this comprehensive site includes a virtual museum, product reviews, classifieds, and much more.

Yahoo! Motorcycles (www.yahoo.com/Business_and_Economy/ Companies/Automotive/Motorcycles/)   Links to motorcycle-related sites.

NEWSGROUPS

Newsgroups are lists of messages to which anyone with an Internet account can subscribe and contribute (or post). Each newsgroup is centered on a particular topic and posted messages are supposed to pertain to that topic, although subscribers do not always follow this guideline. The first three letters of the newsgroup describe one of several broad categories of topics; **rec.** stands for "recreation" and **alt.** stands for "alternative." The rest of the newsgroup name is usually self-explanatory. Be aware that if you post a message to a newsgroup, it is publicly available for anyone to read and may be used by Internet advertisers to send you junk-advertising e-mail messages. See chapter 12, "Internet Basics" for instructions on how to subscribe to newsgroups.

alt.american.automobile
alt.auto.mercedes
alt.auto.parts
alt.auto.parts.wanted
alt.autos
alt.autos.antique
alt.autos.bmw
rec.autos.antique
rec.autos.driving
rec.autos.4x4

rec.autos.makers.chrysler
rec.autos.makers.ford
rec.autos.makers.ford.explorer
rec.autos.makers.ford.mustang
rec.autos.makers.honda
rec.autos.makers.jeep
rec.autos.makers.mazda
rec.autos.makers.mazda.miata
rec.autos.makers.saturn
rec.autos.makers.vw
rec.autos.makers.vw.aircooled
rec.autos.makers.vw.watercooled
rec.autos.marketplace
rec.autos.misc
rec.autos.rod-n-custom
rec.autos.rotary
rec.autos.tech

ORGANIZATIONS

Automobile Association of America (AAA) (www.AAA.com)
This is the online location of AAA, whose membership services include twenty-four-hour roadside assistance, travel services, product and service discounts, vehicle pricing, purchasing, and financing services, approved auto repair directory, insurance services, and Department of Motor Vehicle services.

Automotive Service Association (www.asashop.org) Gives information on car care and finding repair shops. Also discusses how to prepare for accidents and emergencies.

PARTS AND ACCESSORIES

ACDelco Company (www.acdelco.com) The parts supplier knows its parts and has a section warning you to "Beware of Bogus Parts."

A.C.S. America's Car Part Search (www.autopartsused.com)
This site quickly locates used auto parts at great prices.

Any Auto Parts (www.anyautoparts.com)   This online parts supply store located in Alabama lets you submit a form requesting information on parts you need.

Autobahn International Motorsports (www.autobahnint.com)
This site sells performance parts and accessories for most makes and models of cars.

Auto Barn (www.autobarn.com)   This chain of auto parts suppliers based in Long Island, New York, offers an online catalog and encrypted online shopping.

Auto Medic Supply Co. (www.automedicsupply.com)   This Carson, California-based auto supply store allows you to submit a parts request online.

Automotive Air Conditioning Information Server (www.aircondition.com)   Automotive air conditioning information source provides online EPA 609 certification, a/c parts, and literature.

Auto Parts Finder (www.autopartsfinder.com)   Find special interest and antique auto parts here. For restorers and hobbyists.

AutoPro Collector Car Cyber-Center (www.autopro.com)
Online source of vintage, classic, and collector car parts.

Autostyles Home Page (www.autostyles.com)   Sells items to improve your car's style.

Auto Supply Co. (www.autosupplyco.com/index.htm)   This auto parts supplier allows you to submit an online parts request form but it will not accept a form with incomplete automobile information.

Auto Trader Online (www.traderonline.com)   Check out its "Parts & More" section within the vehicle category of your choice to find online parts dealers and service shops.

Auto 2000 (auto2000.com)   Links to auto parts and accessories online.

Auto Value Parts Stores (www.autovalue.com)   The online version of the parts store chain includes catalog, store locations, and technical tips.

AutoZone (www.autozone.com)   Web site for the auto parts store chain.

B&M Racing and Performance Products (www.bmracing.com) This site has catalogs for transmission shifters and drive trains, superchargers, marine engines, light trucks, imports, and racing.

British Parts Connection (www.thebpc.com) Sells quality name brand parts for British sports cars and classics.

California Dream (www.california-dream.com)   Order accessories such as spoilers, truck steps, running boards, bodyside molding, custom striping, and graphics.

Carstuff.com (carstuff.com)   Sells automotive parts, accessories, models, and paraphernalia.

Claus Ettensberger Corporation (www.cecwheels.com)   Stylish European-designed wheels, parts, and accessories. The Web showroom complements its Santa Monica, California, location.

Cyberspace Automotive Performance (www.cyberauto.com) Online automotive performance parts catalog with information on every aspect of owning or driving an automobile.

Discount Tire Direct (www.tires.com)   This site sells all kinds of tires and wheels and it has an interactive wheel system so you can see what a particular style of wheel will look like on your vehicle.

Duragloss Car Care Products (www.spyder.net/duragloss)
Offers many items to keep your car sparkling clean.

East Coast Automotive (www.ecautomotive.com)   Searchable
parts catalog offers secure encrypted online shopping.

eAuto (www.eauto.com)   This "Everything Auto" site contains
links to audio, security, detailing, lighting and safety, sunroof, textile,
interior, and towing products. It also has links to parts and tool manufacturers, and used and salvage parts dealers.

**Edelbrock Performance Products (www.edelbrock.com/edel-
brock.html)**   Order performance parts for motorcycles and automobiles online.

Featherlite Trailers (www.featherlitemfg.com/)   Custom alu-
minum trailers and accessories for cars, trucks, and living quarters.

**Fomoco Obsolete—home of Mustang, Ford, Mercury, Fairlane,
Falcon (www.voicenet.com/~fomoco/)**   Has genuine 1960s
Ford parts.

Gates Rubber Automotive Products (www.gates.com/auto.html)
Includes new product information and technical tips on cooling system belts and hoses.

**Harris Semiconductor Automotive Home Page (www.semi.
harris.com/auto/)**   Sells semiconductors for many automotive
systems.

Image 10 Home Page (www.image10.com)   Describes Image 10
detailing kits to keep new and old vehicles of all kinds looking
shiny-new.

JC Whitney (www.jcwhitneyusa.com)   A premier parts and acces-
sory catalog.

Kanter Auto Products (www.kanter.com)   New mechanical auto
parts for antique 1930–1986 American cars and trucks.

Lingenfelter Performance Engineering (www.lingenfelter.com)
Online catalog of high-performance automotive and marine engines
and components.

**MAZDATRIX for Mazda RX7 & Rotary Engine Parts (www.
mazdatrix.com)**   Online parts and accessories catalog for RX7 and
rotary engines.

**More Than You Ever Wanted to Know About Motor Oil
(vger.rutgers.edu/~ravi/bike/pages/docs/oil.html)**   This automotive enthusiast explains all the different kinds of motor oil on
the market.

Mothers Polishes (mothers.com)   The makers of Carnauba Wax
and other polishes, waxes, and cleaners. The site offers product information as well as car care tips.

MotoMall (www.motomall.com)   This mall lets you shop from
a wide range of vendors of parts, accessories, security equipment,
and more.

PartsVoice (www.partsvoice.com)   For those serious about purchasing auto parts online. Has over 30 million parts in its searchable
database.

Sci.electronics FAQ: Car Battery (www.repairfaq.com)   Provides
a very thorough guide to your car battery.

Sportwing, Inc. (www.sportwing.com)   You can securely order
online spoilers, truck steps, bodyside molding, custom striping, graphics, and other automotive accessories.

Stillen (www.stillen.com)   Manufacturer of high performance automotive parts and accessories. The online counterpart of Steve Millen
Sportsparts, Inc.

Tire Rack (www.tirerack.com)   This site sells high performance
tires and wheels. It has an interactive wheel system to view how a
style of wheel will look on a particular vehicle.

Turtle Wax Home Page (www.turtlewax.com)   Information on car care and detailing that goes beyond the use of Turtle Wax products.

Valvoline (www.valvoline.com)   This motor oil company gives car care tips to both mechanics and drivers.

Van Essen Homepage (www.noord.bart.nl/~essena/)   This is the place to go for parts for German make cars such as Porsche, BMW, Audi, and Volkswagen.

Virtual Auto Parts Store (www.cruzio.com/~vaps/)   This multilingual site has a catalog of discounted name brand car parts and offers worldwide shipping.

Yahoo! Automotive Accessories (www.yahoo.com/Business_and_ Economy/Companies/Automotive/Accessories/index.html) Links to sites offering automotive accessories.

Yahoo! Automotive Parts (www.yahoo.com/Business_and_ Economy/Companies/Automotive/Parts/index.html)   Links to parts suppliers.

PRICE GUIDES

While these sites access the same factory invoice information, they may differ in the timeliness of posting price changes.

AutoSite (www.autosite.com)   AutoSite has a qualified research team that keeps abreast of all regular production automobile models that are released, and assimilates price data quickly into its database. You can perform objective side-by-side comparisons at AutoSite; their reports even include information on insurance rates in your state for the car you've chosen. Try the loan/lease calculator to quickly calculate your monthly payments, annual interest, amortization schedule, and more.

The Car Center (www.intellichoice.com)   For five dollars, this service gives you a report with in-depth information about options, financing, insurance, pricing terminology, and car value versus costs.

CarPrices.com (www.carprices.com)   This site offers inventory prices for new cars and prices for used cars as far back as 1989. It also provides a wide range of automotive information and links.

CarSmart (www.carsmart.com)   Obtain invoice prices on new cars and trucks including customized options. Includes a calculator to determine monthly payments. The site conducts searches for new vehicles not listed.

Edmund's (www.edmunds.com)   Get invoice prices and MSRPs on new and used cars and trucks as well as a comprehensive list of manufacturer's rebates, incentives, and holdbacks. The latter information shows you the additional profit the dealer makes that is not shown on the invoice. This makes Edmund's especially useful compared to sites that merely show invoice prices. The "Price Auto Outlet" offers one-owner, off-lease vehicles direct to Edmund's customers.

Kelley Blue Book (www.kbb.com)   This site is an online version of the venerable used car price guide book. For new vehicles it offers dealer invoice price, manufacturer's suggested retail price, options, standard equipment, and photos. For used vehicles, it helps you determine the fair market value.

REVIEWS

AutoConnect (www.autoconnect.net)   Provides timely news and reviews. The site lets you order automotive books and periodicals through a special link to online bookseller Amazon.com.

AutoSite (www.autosite.com)   Provides reviews as well as other information.

AutoWeek (www.AutoWeek.com) The online version of *AutoWeek* magazine.

Car and Driver (www.caranddriver.com) Includes its up-to-date car reviews and the full text of its buyer's guide. Also offers a map to upcoming car shows, races, and other events.

Car Connection (www.thecarconnection.com) Includes reviews in its "Consumer Driven" section and features "Digital Autobahn," a column about the Internet automotive industry.

The Car Place (www.cftnet.com/members/rcbowden) Robert Bowden has test driven many cars and puts his colloquial reviews on this site.

Cars.com (www.cars.com) Seven major newspaper companies teamed up to create this informational site, which includes model reports, reviews, used car listings, dealer locations, and consumer advice.

CarSmart (www.carsmart.com) Includes many reviews along with pricing information and general automotive advice.

Consumer Reports: Cars and Trucks (www.ConsumerReports. org/Categories/CarsTrucks/index.html) Offers the magazine's car guide and road-test reports and related product reviews.

eAuto (www.eauto.com) "Everything Automotive" includes news and reviews and its newsstand offers discounts on subscriptions to many print automotive publications.

Edmund's (www.edmunds.com) Provides independent information on road tests, comparisons, new and used car reviews, car safety, and crash-tests. Also gives negotiating tips.

Electrifying Times (www.teleport.com/~etimes/) Covers electric vehicles on an international scale.

J. D. Power Guide to Automobiles (www.jdpower.com)   This international market research firm tracks consumer opinion and behavior for a wide range of industries, including the automotive industry.

Microsoft CarPoint (carpoint.msn.com)   Includes new car reviews.

Motor Trend Online (www.motortrend.com)   Has the latest car and truck reviews, repair information, and other auto-related information.

New Car Test Drive (www.nctd.com)   Extensive reviews of new cars and light trucks as well as an archive of reviews from past years.

Popular Mechanics Automotive (popularmechanics.com)   Search by vehicle make and type to find profiles. Includes reviews written by actual owners.

Ride&Drive (www.rideanddrive.com)   An automotive magazine only available in cyberspace. Includes weekly industry updates, road test reports, a column on "Design Disasters" (remember the Pontiac Fiero?) and lots more.

Yahoo! Automotive Magazines (www.yahoo.com/Recreation/ Automotive/News_and_Media/Magazines)   A list of links to a variety of automotive magazine sites.

Yahoo! Automotive Trade Magazines (www.yahoo.com/ Business_and_Economy/Companies/Automotive/Trade_ Magazines/)   These trade magazines may be too technical for the lay reader, but they provide an industry insider's perspective.

SEARCH SITES

Search engines are indexes or directories of Web sites that allow visitors to search for particular words or phrases appearing anywhere on the

Internet. The following search sites each have thorough automotive sections.

AltaVista (www.altavista.digital.com)
DejaNews (www.dejanews.com)   This site is strictly for newsgroups. It allows you to search archived messages pertaining to your topic of interest. "Cars" is one of its main subject categories.
Excite (www.excite.com)
HotBot (www.hotbot.com)
Infoseek (www.infoseek.com)
Lycos (www.lycos.com)
WebCrawler (www.webcrawler.com)
Yahoo! (www.yahoo.com)

SELLING YOUR VEHICLE

Note: See also: "Classifieds"

AutoVantage (www.autovantage.com)   Gives you an estimate of your vehicle's worth when you input its make, model, mileage, and options.

AutoWeb (www.autoweb.com)   Links to pricing guides help you sell your vehicle on this site.

Car-List (www.car-list.com)   You can list your car for $25 on this site.

Classifieds2000 (classifieds2000.com)   This nicely designed site offers free listings.

SERVICE AND REPAIRS

Note: There are a number of Web sites that list and review auto repair shops within specific regions. You can find them through the search sites listed above.

ALLDATA's Automotive Repair Information Internet Site (www.alldata.com)   Provides a wealth of diagnostic and repair information online. Includes factory recall notifications and manufacturers' technical service bulletins (*secret warranties*).

Autobody Online (www.autobodyonline.com)   This site includes repair information about your vehicle as well as a database of over 60,000 autobody shops in North America searchable by city and/or zip code.

AutoDigest Home Page (www.autodigest.com)   This online magazine is for amateurs and professionals interested in automotive repair. It's AutoJob page includes an estimation of how much time common maintenance and repair jobs will take so you can estimate your shop's labor charges. Includes tips to help you tell when a shop is overcharging.

Automotive Resource and Research Center (www.grqnet. com/arrc)   Library of technical books, shop manuals, and service guides for a wide range of vehicles. They will conduct research for you for a fee.

Automotive Service Association (www.asashop.org)   Gives information on car care and finding repair shops. Also discusses how to prepare for accidents and emergencies. Check out their code of ethics.

Automotive Troubleshooting (www2.uic.edu/~msvest1/ trouble.html)   Michael Svesta's homepage includes this guide to solving your car's problems.

Auto Restorer On-Line (www.autorestorer.com)   Includes photos, auto restoration projects, and questions and answers.

AutoSite Garage (www.autosite.com/garage)   AutoSite's section on automotive maintenance, troubleshooting, and repairs contains information and links to useful sites. It takes you step-by-step from identifying symptoms to diagnosing possible causes to fixing the problem.

AUTOSHOP-Online (www.autoshop-online.com)   This site allows you to submit a question about your automotive problem and receive an answer from their master technicians for $29.95. It also gives a free tutorial, "Automotive 101," that details each automotive system.

AutoTech for Windows (www.metacog.com)   This sight sells software to diagnose your automotive troubles.

Auto Trader Online (www.traderonline.com)   Check out the "Parts & More" section within the vehicle category of your choice to find online parts dealers and service shops.

AutoVantage (www.autovantage.com)   Included in its member services are limited free maintenance and repair services from participating Goodyear, Firestone, Meinecke, and Speedy Muffler King service centers.

BBB Consumer Information Series: Tips on Car Repair (www.bbb.org/library/tipscar.html)   Plan ahead with this guide to preventive maintenance and problem solving.

CAP Automotive Information Server (www.cyberauto.com/info/) Cyberspace Automotive Performance's site includes information on roadside assistance programs.

Car Care Council (www.peoplevision.com)   This organization claims to be "the most widely respected source of automotive maintenance and repair information in North America."

CarDocs (cardocs.com)   This site provides diagnosis of your automotive problems for $16.95.

CarTalk.com (www.cartalk.com)   National Public Radio's *Car Talk* show has its own Web site complete with "The Mechan-X Files," a database of repair shops recommended by its listeners. It also includes advice and other tidbits from the show as well as free classified ads.

Detecting a Bad Hose (www.gates.com/squeeze.html)   The Gates Rubber Company informs you how to squeeze your coolant hose.

The Family Car (www.familycar.com)   This site provides information on maintaining your car and dealing with repair shops. It also has a searchable directory of repair shops.

How Cars Work: An Interactive Guide (www.twelvehats.com/ hcw.html)   Twelve Hats Multimedia sells a CD-ROM guide to auto repair and maintenance for Windows.

How to Find Your Way Under the Hood & Around the Car (www.hunter.com/map/e1a.htm)   With perky drawings, this short guide takes you through a checklist of preventive maintenance work you can perform on your vehicle.

Jiffy Lube International (www.jiffylube.com)   The lube job professionals provide store locations and reasons to change your oil.

Midas International (www.midasautosystems.com)   Has a store locator, provides troubleshooting for your braking, exhaust, and suspension sytems, and gives safety tips.

Mile Minder Express (web.wt.net/~clbmmx/)   This is a fee service that will send you regular reminders to perform maintenance on your vehicle.

MotorWeek Online (www.mpt.org/mpt/motorweek)   An online version of the public television show. In addition to its auto reviews, it has "Goss's Garage" for a preventive maintenance schedule for your vehicle.

National Institute for Automotive Service Excellence (www. asecert.org)   This organization was founded to maintain high standards in the automotive service industry. Its site includes a collection of tip sheets for motorists on such subjects as finding a body shop or a repair shop, minimizing pollution, and preparing your car for summer and winter.

Nutz & Boltz Online (www.motorminute.com) This is a Web site for the car radio show, complete with tips on driving and maintenance.

Taking the Scare Out of Auto Repair (www.ftc.gov/bcp/ conline/pubs/autos/autorpr.htm) The FTC's guide to choosing a repair shop.

Wankel Rotary Combustion Engines and Vehicles (www. monito.com/wankel/) This is your guide if you've got a Wankel.

Yahoo! - Automotive: Repairs and Service (www.yahoo.com/ Business_and_Economy/Companies/Automotive/Repairs_and_ Service) Yahoo's directory for auto repairs and service.

VEHICLE IDENTIFICATION NUMBER (VIN) REPORTS

For a fee, the following sites provide vehicle history reports when given the VIN.

Carfax (www.carfax.com)
CarPrices.com (www.carprices.com)
Vinguard (www.vinguard.com)

WARRANTIES

Auto Advantage (www.autowarranties.com) Offers extended warranties and other automobile coverage services for used and new cars.

Auto Service Contracts (www.ftc.gov/bcp/conline/pubs/ autos/autoserv.htm) The Federal Trade Commission's guide to extended warranties.

Auto Warranty Extend (www.svccontracts4less.com) Offers extended warranties and service contracts for new and used cars and trucks.

Buyer's Choice, Inc. (buyerschoicewarranties.com)   Offers warranty protection for used cars.

GLS Development Corporation (www.autoextendwarranty.com) Offers aftermarket extended warranties. Also information on negotiating the purchase of a car.

Interstate National Dealer Services (www.inds.com)   Designs, markets, and administers service contracts and extended warranties.

National Auto Care Corp. (www.natlauto.com)   Provider of vehicle service contracts; offers extended warranties available for several types of automobiles.

Preferred Warranties, Inc. (www.prefwarranty.com)   Provides extended service contracts for used cars and trucks sold through independent dealers.

Warranty Central (www.gmwarrantycentral.com)   Sells GM protections plans and warranties.

Warranty Direct (www.warrantydirect.com)   Provides extended service contracts direct from the insurer.

Warranty Gold (www.warrantygold.com)   This provider of extended warranties claims they'll save you up to 60 percent off your dealership's warranty plan by cutting out the middleman.

Wholesale Auto Experts (www.wbfx.com/wae/)   Sells wholesale auto warranties for new or used vehicles.

Glossary

100 percent sale: A ploy used by dealerships to sell new cars by promising to pay buyers 100 percent of the original selling price of their trade-in, minus costs for repairs and reconditioning. Those costs will usually be grossly inflated to reduce the buy-back price to less than what car owners could get by selling their trade-in themselves.

acquisition fee: See *assignment fee*.

add-ons: A variety of extra items and services that the dealership offers in addition to what the factory installs in the vehicle. The charges for these are often grossly inflated above their cost to the dealership.

ADP: An add-on that secretly means "Additional Dealer Profit" but gives the customer no value.

annual percentage rate (APR): The percentage of interest that is effectively charged per year on the principal of a loan. The federal Truth-in-Lending Act requires the APR to be disclosed in large bold type on any consumer loan agreement.

APR: See *annual percentage rate*.

assignment fee: A fee charged by the leasing company to pay for commissions earned by the dealership. Also called an acquisition fee, lease inception fee, or lease initiation fee.

auto broker: A service that facilitates automotible sales by bringing buyers together with participating sellers. Also called an auto buying service.

auto-buying service: See *auto broker*.

back-end profit: The dealership's profit derived from financing, insurance, and add-ons.

bait and switch: Advertising a particular vehicle at an attractively low price to lure a customer into the dealership, then disparaging the advertised vehicle (or claiming it is unavailable) and switching the customer to one with a higher profit margin. The Federal Trade Commission and many state statutes prohibit this tactic.

balloon payment: A final loan payment that is greater than preceding payments.

base price: The price of a vehicle without options or other charges added.

basic warranty: A guarantee that the vehicle will perform as promised or repairs will be made free of charge for any defects caused by the manufacturer. Each warranty has its own terms and limitations, including a maximum time or mileage limit on its coverage.

blind trade: Agreeing to pay a price for a used car based on a description of it rather than an actual inspection. Often made conditionally, pending confirmation of the accuracy of the description.

book out: To calculate the resale value of your vehicle using a price guide book or Web site.

book the trade: Paying the wholesale price for a vehicle listed in one of the standard price guides such as *Edmund's or Kelley Blue Book*.

book value: The fair market value of a car as listed in *Kelley Blue Book*. See *high blue book* and *low blue book*.

browser: An application that allows you to navigate and view Web pages. Popular browsers are Netscape Navigator and Microsoft Internet Explorer.

building the reserve: When a dealership increases the percentage rate charged to a customer on an auto loan beyond the lending institution's fair market rate, it splits the additional profit with the lender.

bump: After a customer has agreed to a tentatively offered price, the dealership reneges, promising that the deal can only be concluded if the customer agrees to pay more. This is *bumping* up the price. Also called a *raise*.

business manager: Actually a car dealership salesperson specializing in closing a sale and including as much back-end profit as possible. Also called a finance manager or a financial counselor.

buyer's order: A sales contract to purchase a vehicle.

cap cost: See *capitalization cost*.

capitalization cost: The negotiated price of a vehicle used to calculate a lease.

capitalization cost reduction: A down payment, which reduces the price of the vehicle, and the size of the monthly payments on a lease.

cap reduction: See *capitalization cost reduction*.

chat room: An area online where you can chat with other members in real time.

close: To get a customer to sign a contract.

closed-end lease: A lease at the end of which the lessee is not responsible for any difference between a vehicle's initially estimated residual value and its actual appraised value. Because the lessee assumes none of this risk, monthly payments are usually higher than those of an open-end lease.

cookie: A string of characters that a Web site inserts into an Internet browser's cookie file on the user's hard drive. This allows a site to track the user's movements through the site and any return visits. The site operators may build a consumer profile of the user and target advertisements to the user's assumed interests. Operators also use cookies to store user passwords for more convenient re-entry into the site.

corporate invoice: See *manufacturer's invoice.*

corporate representative: An individual who acts as a liaison to franchised dealerships for an automotive manufacturer.

corrosion perforation warranty: A manufacturer's warranty guaranteeing the integrity of a vehicle's exterior against rusting for a limited time.

dealer: May refer to an entire dealership or just its owner.

dealer incentive: An incentive, usually money, that a manufacturer gives to a dealership to motivate it to sell more of a particular model of vehicle. Also see *holdback.*

dealer invoice: See *manufacturer's invoice.*

dealer prep: An extra charge dealers try to include that purports to cover expenses incurred to prepare the vehicle for sale, but is actually pure profit.

depreciation: The loss of a vehicle's value, whether due to wear and tear, obsolescence, or external factors.

destination charge: The cost of transporting a vehicle from the factory to a dealership.

disposition fee: A fee charged in some auto leases to lessees who do not exercise their option to buy at the end of the lease term.

domain name: The part of an Internet Web address between the "**http://**" and the first forward slash (/). The domain name's suffix can tell you what type of site it is: **.com** (commercial), **.edu** (education), **.gov** (government), **.net** (network), **.org** (organization).

download: To electronically transfer a file from one computer to another, e.g. from a Web site to your computer's hard drive.

drive-off: A fee charged in some auto leases that may include the first month's payment, tax, and license fees to be paid up front as an unacknowledged down payment.

drivetrain warranty: See *powertrain warranty*.

DVF: An add-on that secretly means "Dealer Vacation Fund" that provides the consumer no additional value.

early termination fee: A fee charged to the lessee for breaking an auto lease before the end of its full term.

easy sell: A customer who does not have any sales resistance.

e-mail: Electronic mail is a means by which anyone with an electronic address may correspond with anyone else—whether down the street or across the plantet—also possessing such an address. E-mail can be exchanged within a private computer network or across the Internet.

encryption: A method of scrambling electronic data so that it may not be read by anyone other than the sender and the recipient. Used for creating a secure environment for online transactions.

excess mileage fee: A fee that the lessee pays at the conclusion of the auto lease for any mileage accrued above a specified annual maximum. The fee is usually calculated as number of cents per excess miles.

extended warranty: Coverage to provide repair and maintenance work for a vehicle after its manufacturer's warranty expires. It generally costs much more than what you would pay for service as you need it. Also called a maintenance contract or service contract.

F&I department: The finance and insurance department of a dealership.

factory invoice: See *manufacturer's invoice.*

factory rebate: A payment manufacturers give to buyers for choosing a particular vehicle being promoted.

FAQ: See *frequently asked questions.*

finance manager: See *business manager.*

financial counselor: See *business manager.*

flipping the deal: A tactic used in dealerships to keep potential customers by transferring them from one salesperson to another.

floor planning: When dealerships display cars that they do not own but keep on credit from financial institutions.

frequently asked questions (FAQ): A list of commonly asked questions and answers about a particular subject.

front-end profit: The dealership's profit derived from the difference between the selling price of the vehicle and what the dealership actually paid for it.

GAP insurance: Insurance that covers the difference between what your automotive insurance provides and what you must pay if your leased vehicle is stolen or damaged in an accident.

general manager: The boss at a dealership, who reports to the owner and is in charge of overseeing all of the departments, including new car sales, used car sales, parts, and service.

goodwill service: See *secret warranty*.

high blue book: The retail rather than wholesale price for a used car as listed in *Kelley Blue Book*.

holdback: Money a manufacturer gives to a dealer for each vehicle it sells, which is not included on the invoice of the vehicle's cost to the dealership. Also called a kickback.

HTML: See *HyperText Markup Language*.

HTTP: See *HyperText Transfer Protocol*.

hyperlink: Any portion of a Web page that, when you click on it, sends you to another Web page. Text hyperlinks are usually underlined and in color. The color of a hyperlink changes after you have visited the linked site, so you can keep track of where you've been.

HyperText Markup Language (HTML): The programming code that provides formatting instructions so that World Wide Web sites can be viewed by browser programs.

HyperText Transfer Protocol (HTTP): When opening a World Wide Web location, it used to be necessary to type "**http://**" in front of a Web address in order to specify that you were seeking a site on the World Wide Web as opposed to other kinds of sites that do not use HTML. Newer Web browsers make this unnecessary.

icon: In Internet parlance, an icon is a small graphic or symbol that represents an application, command, file, or other option.

in the bucket: When the amount that a vehicle owner must pay off in loans is greater than the true wholesale value of that vehicle, the owner is in the bucket. Also called being upside down.

Internet: A globally interconnected complex of computer networks that grew out of a U.S. government-sponsored linkage of universities and agencies.

invoice: See *manufacturer's invoice.*

Internet service provider (ISP): A company that provides computer users access to the Internet and an e-mail address.

ISP: See *Internet Service Provider.*

kickback: See *holdback.*

lay down: A customer who has no sales resistance, who "lays down" and accepts extra charges that salespeople add on to a vehicle's cost rather than fighting them.

lease: A contract granting the use of a vehicle for a specified time in exchange for payment.

lease inception fee: See *assignment fee.*

lease initiation fee: See *assignment fee.*

lease term: The length of time the lessee contracts to have use of a vehicle.

lemon laws: Federal and state laws that offer redress for consumers who have bought vehicles with defects.

lessee: The party in a lease who pays to use a vehicle for a specified time but does not own the vehicle.

lessor: The owner of the vehicle leased to a lessee. May be an automotive manufacturer's leasing subsidiary, an investment company, or a bank.

list price: See *manufacturer's suggested retail price.*

loss leader: A vehicle or other automotive product or service offered at a retailer's cost or less to attract customers.

lowball: An offer to buy or sell at an unrealistically low price. Sellers do this to get customers to return; buyers do this to initiate a tough negotiation.

low blue book: The wholesale rather than retail price for a used car as listed in *Kelley Blue Book*.

maintenance contract: See *extended warranty*.

manufacturer's invoice: The list of prices that a manufacturer charges a dealer for a particular vehicle and its various options, destination charges and regional advertising assessments.

manufacturer's invoice price (MIP): The total of all the prices on a manufacturer's invoice that apply to a particular vehicle with the options a customer chooses.

manufacturer's suggested retail price (MSRP): The inflated price listed on the sticker on the vehicle at the dealership. Internet price guides provide comparisons between the MSRP and the manufacturer's invoice for a vehicle and its options. Also known as sticker price or list price, some cynics call it the "manufacturer's suggested rip-off price."

margin: The profit derived from what a dealer charges for a vehicle above what it actually cost.

market price: The retail price or *high blue book* value of a used car.

market value: What the fair going rate for a used vehicle is on the market. Also refers to what *Edmund's Price Guide* calls a used vehicle's retail price.

MIP: See *manufacturer's invoice price*.

money factor: A number used in leasing to calculate the annual percentage rate of interest built into the lease without having to admit that there is interest. It may be converted into an approximation of the APR by multiplying by 24.

mooch: An insulting term some car salespeople use to refer to customers who are easily manipulated.

MSRP: See *manufacturer's suggested retail price.*

Net, the: Short for Internet.

newsgroup: A newsgroup is an online discussion group. On the Internet, there are literally thousands of newsgroups covering every conceivable topic.

open-end lease: In contrast to a *closed-end* lease, the lessee may have to pay a substantial amount at the end of this lease if the initially calculated residual value overestimated the actual appraised market value of the vehicle when the lease is terminated. Because the lessee assumes this risk, the monthly payments on an open-end lease are usually lower than those for a closed-end lease.

option to buy: A clause in a lease that allows the lessee to purchase the vehicle at the end of the lease's term. This is invariably more expensive than obtaining a loan up front to purchase the vehicle.

photo bubble technology: Allows users to view a 360-degree panoramic view of a scene, such as a vehicle's interior. With the mouse you can spin around inside these three-dimensional creations.

plug-in: Plug-in applications are programs that can easily be installed and used as part of your Web browser. Popular plug-ins include RealAudio, Adobe Acrobat Reader, and Macromedia's Shockwave, an interactive animation and sound player.

policy adjustment: See *secret warranty.*

pounder: If a customer is willing to pay $1,000 in extra profits tacked on to a vehicle's price, he or she is known as a pounder. A two-pounder accepts $2,000 extra, a three-pounder accepts $3,000, and so on.

powertrain warranty: A manufacturer's warranty that guarantees the performance of a vehicle's engine, transmission, and rear axle. Also called a drivetrain warranty.

protection package: An add-on that can include such protective measures as rustproofing, undercoating, glazing or fabric conditioning. New cars rarely need such additional protections, especially at the highly inflated prices dealers charge.

Quicktime VR (virtual reality): Software that may be downloaded from the Internet and *plugged in* to a Web browser program to allow users to circle around a photographed object as well as zoom in or out of the picture.

raise: See *bump*.

recall: An official announcement made by a manufacturer that a vehicle has a defect that must be fixed or replaced free of charge to the owner.

reserve: The difference between the interest rate that a dealership charges a customer and what the lending bank considers a fair market rate.

residual value: The estimate of the value that a leased car will retain at the end of a lease, expressed as a percentage of the MSRP.

retail price: The price at which used car dealerships are selling a vehicle, as opposed the lower wholesale price that they are willing to pay for it.

sales manager: A senior salesperson who has years of practice in overcoming customer objections and boosting profit margins. Often, the person to whom the initial salesperson *turns over* or *flips* a customer.

salvaged vehicle: A vehicle that was refurbished after being declared a total loss due to an accident or other serious damage.

search engine: Indexes or directories of Web sites that allow visitors to search for particular words or phrases appearing anywhere on the Internet. Popular search engines include Yahoo! (**www.yahoo.com**), AltaVista (**www.altavista.digital.com**), and WebCrawler (**www.webcrawler.com**).

secret warranty: Manufacturers authorize free repairs of potentially defective parts not covered by a recall or the basic warranty, but only if the vehicle owner complains about the problem. Officially called a technical service bulletin (TSB). Also known as a goodwill service or a policy adjustment.

secure online transaction: A purchase made over the Internet in which the credit information that a buyer transmits is encrypted, or scrambled, so that only the seller can decipher it.

service adjustment warranty: A warranty that provides free corrections of minor problems like squeaks, rattles, and misalignment.

slash-it sale: A high-pressure sales gimmick in which prices are publicly slashed, creating a frenzied environment in which buyers jump at deals they think are great bargains.

slow pay: A person who has gotten behind on credit repayment.

spamming: A form of online junk mail, in which advertisers send messages indiscriminately to vast numbers of recipients via e-mail and newsgroup postings.

special value package: An add-on that merely increases the dealer's profit without giving the buyer any additional value. Often placed on the stickers of hot import car models.

steal the trade: When a used car dealer pays a good deal less than a vehicle's wholesale value.

sticker price: See *manufacturer's suggested retail price*.

subvented rate: Car loan interest rate that manufacturers subsidize to an artificially low level to draw in customers. Usually includes restrictions that keep monthly payments high enough to discourage many people from opting for it.

surfing the Net: Using an Internet browser program to explore the World Wide Web, often by clicking on various *hyperlinks* that take you from one Web page to another.

switch: A sales tactic to get you to shift from the vehicle you are considering to one that better serves the seller's purposes (e.g. by providing a higher profit margin).

technical service bulletin: See *secret warranty*.

title and registration fees: Fees imposed by state motor vehicle departments when you take ownership of a vehicle and register it with the state.

T.O.: See *turn over*.

trade-in allowance: The amount of money a dealer pays you for your current vehicle, which is deducted from what you must pay for the vehicle you are buying. Usually a good deal less than what you could get if you sold your current vehicle yourself.

trade-in value: The term *Edmund's Price Guide* uses for a used car's wholesale price.

turn over (T.O.): A sales tactic in which customers are kept on the lot by being "turned over" to a new salesperson.

uniform resource locator (URL): The technical name for the location or address of a Web site, e.g. **http://www.cyberwheels.com**.

unwind: A vehicle that must be returned to a dealership within ten days of contracting because the customer listed false information on the credit application or a bank could not be found to underwrite the loan.

upside down: See *in the bucket*.

URL: See *uniform resource locator*.

vehicle identification number (VIN): The unique series of numbers and letters assigned to a car that identifies it. The VIN is found on the passenger side dashboard and elsewhere in a vehicle.

VIN: See *vehicle identification number*.

Web address: Also known as the URL, the means by which a user locates a Web site on the Internet.

Web site: All the collected documents that are integrated at a particular Web address. You can tell that a hyperlink took you to a different Web site when the *domain name* of the address changes.

wholesale price: The price that the dealer market is paying for a used car, which is below the retail price at which dealers will resell it.

World Wide Web (WWW): The portion of the Internet, now dominant, which allows users to access increasingly sophisticated combinations of text, graphics, moving images, and sound. Software applications can run within Internet browsers that allow users to interact with Web sites in a variety of ways.

Index

About the Authors

 **Ron Raisglid** A graduate of Cornell University, Ron Raisglid entered the automotive industry to help support himself through college. After ten years in conventional automotive sales, he became one of the first advocates of Internet car sales in 1997. Ron's career in Internet automotive sales was launched when a Toyota dealership hired him to design their Internet program. A consultant to dealerships, manufacturers, and auto brokers, Ron was inspired to write this book after helping friends and associates purchase cars online at amazingly low prices.

Cheri Turner is an independent film producer living in Los Angeles.

William Mikulak is a writer and research consultant living in Los Angeles. He received a Ph.D. from the Annenberg School for Communication at the University of Pennsylvania.